DATE DUE

My Dear Mollie

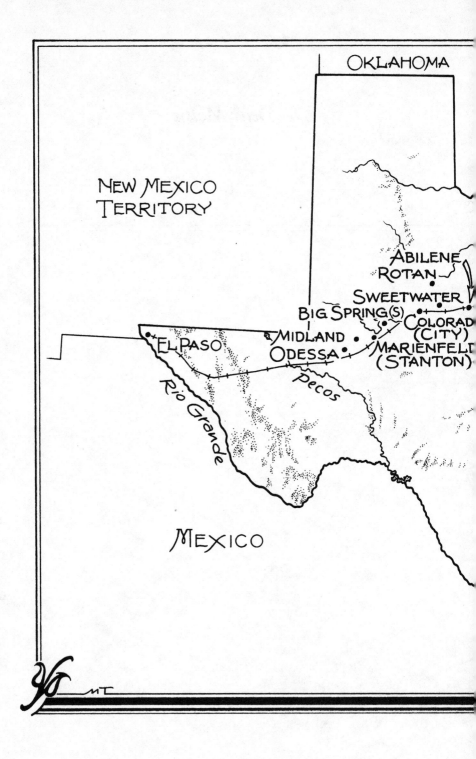

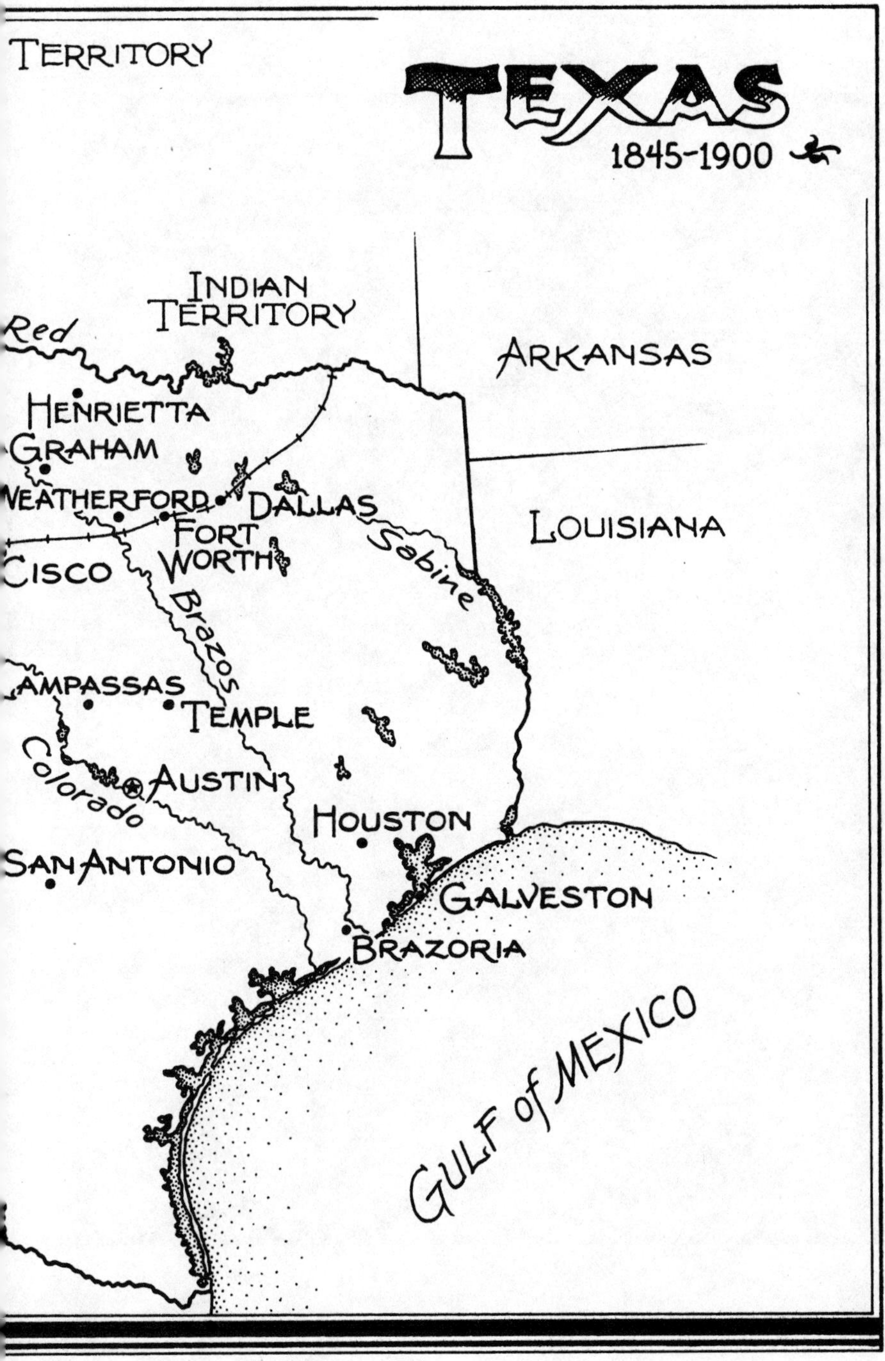

TERRITORY

TEXAS
1845-1900

INDIAN
TERRITORY

ARKANSAS

Red

HENRIETTA
GRAHAM
WEATHERFORD
DALLAS
FORT
WORTH

CISCO

Brazos

Sabine

LOUISIANA

AMPASSAS
TEMPLE

Colorado

AUSTIN

SAN ANTONIO

HOUSTON

GALVESTON
BRAZORIA

GULF of MEXICO

My
Dear Mollie

Love Letters of a Texas Sheep Rancher

Collected by his Granddaughter

Agnesa Reeve

Hendrick-Long Publishing Co.
Dallas

Library of Congress Cataloging in Publication Data

My dear Mollie : love letters of a Texas sheep rancher / collected by
his granddaughter, Agnesa Reeve.
   p. cm.
   Summary: A collection of late nineteenth-century letters by a
Texas sheep rancher to his sweetheart in which he reveals the
painful loneliness of life on the plains.
   ISBN 0-937460-62-1
   1. Ranch life—Texas, West—History—19th century. 2. Reeve.
Agnesa—correspondence. 3. Texas, West—Social life and customs.
4. Sheep ranchers—Texas, West—correspondence. [1. Ranch life-
-Texas—History. 2. Texas—Social life and customs. 3. Sheep
ranchers—corresponsence. 4. Letters.] I. Reeve, Agnesa.
F391.M9 1990   90-41891
976.4'092'—dc20   CIP
                                                                          AC

© 1990 Agnesa Reeve

Design and Production
Joanna Hill Design   Santa Fe, New Mexico

Hendrick-Long Publishing Co.
Dallas, Texas 75225

Contents

Preface

The structure of a family, or of a romance, is not the same at the end of the twentieth century as it was at the end of the nineteenth. *My Dear Mollie*, a collection of letters written by a suitor to his sweetheart between December 1888 and March 1890 illustrates a few of the prevailing social attitudes.

In the first place, the father of a family had total authority. The example in this narrative is extreme, but in most families it was expected that children obey without question. This expectation did not cease when the children became adults. The position was, Father makes the decisions because Father knows best. Of course, in this instance, Father is a judge, so understandably he considers that his word is law.

In the second place, many children faced the advent of a step-mother. Wives often had a baby every year or two, and many young women did not survive to see their children grow up. A father was likely to marry again, providing a stepmother for his existing family and increasing it. Sometimes this was a happy development for the "first" children, and sometimes it was not.

Whether first wife or fourth, a woman was not to be considered the intellectual equal of her husband. It was an era when men, almost without exception, assumed their own superiority. English novelist George Eliot (pseudonym of Mary Ann Evans), satirizing this attitude in *Middlemarch* (1871) says, "A man's mind—what there is of it—has always the advantage of being masculine. . .and even his ignorance is of a sounder quality."

Families were larger than they are now, so there were a great many aunts, uncles, and cousins, who tended to keep in communication with each other. Support, advice, and criticism were readily offered concerning everyone's affairs, whether such comment was requested or not. (Cousins and aunts still do this, of course, but in the late 1800s there were so many cousins and aunts!)

All of these factors influenced the relationships between young men and women. A parent's disapproval of a swain inevitably cast a blight on romance, and might well destroy it. A girl used to obeying her father cringed at the thought of incurring his displeasure. The opinions of members of the extended family also would have been made apparent, for good or ill.

If the female was rated low in intellect, she was rated high in delicacy, to be handled with ostentatious care, at least in theory. She was to be subjected to neither coarse language nor unpleasant facts. In response, she tried to adhere to what seems now an unnatural and stifling pattern of behavior. Both men and women were inclined to put the objects of their affection on pedestals, endowing them with impossibly high principles and expecting inhumanly perfect behavior.

In spite of all this, however, people did fall in love and marry. It may be that a courtship through letters worked as well as one conducted in person. Because it involved only two people, and bypassed some of the hampering conventions, perhaps it encouraged a better understanding.

The letters in this volume are love letters, persuasive, exultant, or despondent, depending on the mood of the author. For most of the period the correspondence covers, the writer is in the sheep business in sparsely settled West Texas, and the letters make apparent not only his longing for his sweetheart, but the painful loneliness of life on the plains. It is a record of a particular time and place, and of a romance then, and there.

Introduction

Great and impersonal forces—the attack of storm and flood, the price of cotton and livestock, the rise and fall of nations—affect the lives of the people who live through them, just as do personal triumphs and disasters. In the last decades of the nineteenth century, Texas was recovering from the chaos of the Civil War (a war which would have been referred to as "The War Between the States" by the Texans in this book), and wide-ranging changes were taking place, such as the building of the railroad.

Among the developments assisted by the railroad was the growth of new towns in West Texas, towns whose inhabitants were likely to be in the livestock business, raising either cattle or sheep. It was the sheep business in the West Texas town of Midland that would have an impact on the future of a baby born on October 7, 1866, in Brazoria, Texas, some 500 miles to the southeast.

The baby was christened Mary, but always called Mollie. When Mollie McCormick was only four years old, her mother died. Besides Mollie, five other small children were left motherless by the death of Mary Jane Copes McCormick—four older than Mollie and one younger, two-year-old Andrew.

About a year after the loss of Mary Jane, the children's father, District Judge Andrew Phelps McCormick, married again. This wife would bear eleven children and survive to an irascible old age.

If, when he married again, the father thought to provide his orphaned children with maternal care, he sadly missed his objective, for the stepmother had little interest and no sympathy for the bereaved youngsters. (The second Mrs. McCormick was apparently devoid of sympathy for anyone. Only one example of this lack is that years later, when a broken hip made her husband an invalid, it was one or another of his daughters who cared for him, not his wife.)

In spite of this unpleasant situation, Mollie and the other children managed, partly by loyal support of each other. One thing that enlivened their life in Brazoria was a series of visits to Austin during legislative sessions, as McCormick was a member of the Texas Senate from 1876 to 1879. On one occasion when Mollie accompanied her father to a legislative session in the old capitol building, she was puzzled by his bustling about, ostentatiously propping up the balcony of the Senate chamber. When she asked him what he was doing, he explained that the senators wanted a new capitol.

If he intended to be humorous, this is one of the few even slightly light-hearted episodes that are remembered of this stern gentleman. More characteristic is the report of his sitting in church flanked by his children, with his arms outstretched along the back of the pew, the better to dig his thumb into the shoulder of any child who squirmed.

Judge McCormick's mother lived in Brazoria with the family and, of course, when they went to their beach cottage on the coast some twenty miles away, she went along. It was at this beach house, on September 15, 1875, that she died. The next morning, as her body lay in state in the parlor, the sky and sea began to turn an ominous dirty green, heralding a storm. Within hours a hurricane struck.

As the wind raged, the water rose until it surrounded the house. At the last minute possible, the Judge sent his family to safety, but refused to go himself, insisting that he would not leave his mother's body. Finally, when the water was at its peak and about to sweep back out, always the most powerful and dangerous force of a tidal wave, the sheriff rowed his boat up to the front porch once more and insisted McCormick leave. The Judge finally nodded and went inside. When he came back out he was carrying his mother's body. He put it into the boat, climbed in himself, and they hastily paddled to high ground.

The house was swept entirely away. When they returned to see

Mollie McCormick in a picture made in Waukesha, Wisconsin, where the family vacationed. Date of the photograph is unknown.

what damage there had been to the cottage, the only thing left to mark the site was a chamber pot.

In Brazoria, the children's schooling was conducted in private classes made up either of just family members (certainly there were enough of them) or including neighbors. In addition, their father administered a reading program in which each child read assigned material during the day and was questioned on it that evening. As a result of this exercise, or in spite of it, Mollie became a voracious reader.

The McCormicks varied their social life with frequent visits to Austin, where there was a large family connection. In fact, the town seems to have been peopled with "cousins" and "aunts." It was on such a visit in 1872 that six-year-old Mollie first met a young man who was a distant cousin, John Barclay McGill. She would not see him again for seven years, and then in only a brief encounter at a family gathering.

In 1879 the family moved to Dallas, where McCormick was to serve as judge of the northern district. They lived in the Oak Cliff section, and Mollie was enrolled in a private school there. To escape the heat, they spent summers in the lake district of Wisconsin. Waukesha boasted the mineral springs that were a popular feature of nineteenth century spas, and even young girls walked down the path to the spring to drink probably very unpleasant, though healthful, waters.

A few years later in 1882, the family moved again, this time to Graham, Texas. Graham was Mollie's "home," although she soon left for college at Western Female Seminary in Oxford, Ohio. Included in her gear for college was her sterling table silver. To guard against loss, it was engraved on the back with her full name.

During her college years, vacations were likely to be spent in Wisconsin, or visiting friends, rather than in Graham. It was a congenial life, in spite of dauntingly rigid rules of what constituted ladylike behavior. For example, at one house party attended by several particularly handsome young men, Mollie refrained from eating the crisp toast at breakfast because it crunched excessively, and such an indelicate noise would certainly disgust the gentlemen.

After a delay of a year when she was kept at home, either because she had fainted at some discussion of blood, or because her father wanted her graduation to coincide with her younger sister Sallie's, Mollie graduated from the Seminary in 1887.

For the next three years Mollie lived in Graham, helping care for the numerous small children still at home, enduring an unamiable step-mother, and personifying the role of dutiful daughter to an exacting and dictatorial parent. But in the middle of that period, in the winter of 1888 when Mollie was twenty-two, something happened that would sow a seed of rebellion.

That December the McCormicks made a visit to Austin to attend a family wedding, and another cousin was also there, John McGill. The romance that began then (at least on one side) was destined to follow a rocky road. Its progress is chronicled in the letters J.B.M. wrote, first to "My Dear Cousin," but soon to "My Dear Mollie," and then "My Dear Little Girl."

❧ I ❧

My Dear Cousin

Miss Mollie McCormick
908 San Antonio
Austin, Texas

New Central Hotel,
Mrs. R. R. and N.A. Pepper, Proprietresses,
Eighth St. and Avenue D.
Temple, Texas.
Dec. 19, 1888

My Dear Cousin,

When I told you yesterday evening that I should wait a week before writing, I at least thought that I could stand it until I reached my destination, but you perceive I was wrong. Discovering that a delay of four hours was necessary at this point it occurred to me that nothing could make the time pass more swiftly than to hold "sweet converse" with you. Under the circumstances it has to be done without the "aid of either lips *or* tongue" and thus proving that the Poet had not investigated this matter thoroughly.

The wedding is over but my suffering still continues. I had to ride fifty miles with the "happy couple," and on reaching this point I have shut them in the parlor for safekeeping, while I am occupying the office with one eye fixed on the parlor door. The only thing tending to interrupt the solemnity of the marriage ceremony was, the groom thinking the minister was making him promise too much, stopped him in the middle of his questions to answer "I will," but after reconsidering the matter agreed to say "I will" again after the "parson" had finished.

I have been doing more solid thinking during the last three days than I can remember indulging in for several years, and on a subject heretofore entirely remote. A very great change has come "over the spirit of my dream" since Saturday evening, for which you are responsible. I have always been guilty of procrastination in everything and the consequence is that I left many things unsaid which are now struggling in my mind for relief. Possibly they *may* be said more intelligently on paper than by word of mouth, or as I read somewhere without the "assistance of the tongue." I discover myself now in a situation where I very seldom get, one where I need a few instructions.

I have embarked on a river of liking, drifting with a rapidly increasing current toward the ocean of love and you will have to act as pilot. Tell me now before I float any further what may be the result, whether it lies within my power with every exertion I am capable of making, to finally anchor in the harbor of *your* love or will I be hopelessly stranded on the rocks of your indifference.

Well, I guess I had better "slack up" a little. The foregoing sentimental effusion proves almost too much for my constitution, and a few more lines might cause you a second fainting spell, but I have a continual struggle to keep an upper hand on my poetic nature and it will sometimes crop out in spite of all I can do.

Leaving all joking aside, however, you have it in your power to make me exceedingly happy, or cause me to regret having written this and allowed myself the pleasure of indulging in a very pleasant dream. I don't ask you for any binding contract, but unless my case is absolutely hopeless, I will set myself to win your regard, and what I undertake, I have the satisfaction of knowing that I very seldom fail to accomplish. Although this venture is in a different direction from those I usually follow, with your permission I will try to reach the harbor "heretofore stated."

Unless I receive from you some slightly encouraging reply, I do not think it would add any to my peace of mind to visit Austin soon or to carry on a very extensive correspondence. I know you are too true a woman to take any pleasure in leading a fellow on and finally landing him on the "rocks of your indifference" "before mentioned."

This is my first attempt at a composition of this kind; if it doesn't meet your approval in its general construction, you are perfectly welcome to criticize it as severely as you will, provided you give a favorable answer. Otherwise have a little mercy, and at least let me think that I have done credit to myself on paper.

You will not need to be told that after this is posted, I will be rather mentally unsettled until I hear from you. As I like to have my brain to some extent under my own control, you will realize that a quick answer will be appreciated.

If I haven't indulged in much sentiment it's for two reasons. The first is that I do not think you like it, the second that I have never practiced sentimentality enough to be proficient in its use. But I think you can learn if you have a mind to, that a man without much romance can love as much and as long as one with it.

One request I have to make on closing and it is this: please don't use the expression "I will always be your friend but can never be anything else." I never had it used toward me and if possible would like to go through life without it.

Yours (insert anything here that you desire. I can fill it in next time)

J.B.M.

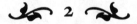

The Lampasas Leader,
Lampasas, Texas.
Dec. 24, 1888

My Dear Mollie,

As "business is business" I'm going to address you in a business-like manner. You will p pase to observe the accent on the possessive pronoun. I have omitted the title of relationship.

I received your letter about two hours ago. I waited with commendable impatience at the P.O. last night until the mail was distributed and then wandered out into the darkness bearing with me the same load of fear and uncertainty that I had been laboring under since Wednesday. Tonight I went to the depot long before the train came in and injured my eyes looking down the R.R. track watching for the headlight of the engine. If my eyesight troubles me any in the future years, I shall attribute the cause of it to this night's anxiety and expect you to feel as if I deserved some consideration at your hands.

John Barclay McGill in a photograph of unknown date.

When I was at last rewarded by taking a letter from the box with the Austin postmark, I suddenly discovered that my impatience had altogether departed and it was with fear and trembling, figuratively speaking, that I finally "broke the seal" and proceeded to "devour" its contents.

I have memorized it and yet do not know if I can exactly locate myself.

I fully realize one fact. It has often occurred to me since I saw you in '82, and it is this. Why, when I first knew you when a little girl, did I not make you love me so well that your affection would have lasted 'till now?

I remember so well the first time I ever saw you. Where was my guardian angel at that moment that it was not whispered in my ear, "This little girl will be a woman grown in a few short years?" The second time we met you say I treated you kindly! I wish the days could be recalled and I could live over again that period of my life. As it is I feel very thankful toward the "aforesaid" angel that my treatment of you was such as to cause you, ten years after, to remember it gratefully.

Since our third meeting you have been frequently in my thoughts, but a rather small opinion of myself (sounds unreasonable doesn't it!) and a very exalted one of you has kept down any aspirations like those I allow myself to indulge in at the present. I had been with you a very little while the last time, before I made up my mind, without my opinion of either of us changing, that "whereas" very few men deserve the affection of a woman, they, nevertheless, often *win* it. "Resolved, therefore," that I would endeavor to be one of those men.

You say that you have reached the venerable age of twenty-two years without feeling any of the peculiar sensations which are called love. If you will remember that I am a little more than ten years your senior, I believe you would be somewhat more considerate in your remarks concerning age.

I have reached this patriarchal stage of my existence without having to regret much wasted affection of this kind, and still I'm hopeful. If my sentiment toward you is not something of this character, I will admit then that my constitution is such that I am destined to go through life without it.

You don't seem to have fully understood my allusions to the pilot business. I was afraid if "I drifted into poetry" 'twould be too much like Browning, but I tried to make it plain. I simply wanted to know what hope you could hold out to me, that I could make you care for me as I did for you. If I remember rightly you told me, during the last few minutes of our closing conversation, that it would require no great effort on your part to do this.

I did not think then that you knew how far I had "drifted."

Your letter might have been more encouraging, but it might also have been a blow to me that would have hurt more than you imagine. I feel much better than I did a few hours ago.

If I think it *worth my while* to expend my energies in trying to gain the first place in your affections, My Dear Girl, if I could convince you how I value that place, you would not doubt that I consider it worth my while.

I cannot, if I would, go off into any rapturous strain of adoration and love. I have sometimes regretted that this element was left out in my makeup and that I was so different from others. But since I have become to some extent acquainted with your character, I'm inclined to flatter myself that we have one trait in common. That if my letters to, or conversations with, you are not overflowing with sentiment, yours will have no advantage over mine, and neither of us will have any reason to complain, nor will we appreciate each other less.

Don't get the idea from the foregoing, that I do not give each of us credit for being able to feel these things as deeply as anyone, but simply we are incapable of being "soft." The word "love" has been used so often and so long, that I would like to discover something to take its place. I often refrain from the use of it and notice in your letter that it does not occur often.

I realize that I have one difficulty to overcome, caused by your visit among the members of my own immediate family. This is a subject always distasteful to me, but which in justice to myself I must touch on. Do not let the surroundings and affairs there influence you in the slightest against me.* I have stood alone for several years, and whether or not I succeed in this the one great wish of my life, I shall I hope continue to stand alone as regards individuality. As I told you, the girl that honors me with her preference shall never have occasion to regret it on account of my kin . . . .

My own movements in the immediate future are hard to determine upon. Until I had seen you I was quietly drifting along, not giving much thought to what I should do, and taking things as they came. You have rendered this course impossible any longer, but all my attention since I left Austin has been so taken up in speculation, in regard to what reply you would make to my letter, that I've had no time to think about anything else.

I must try to get down to see you again before a great while, because altho' letter writing is better than silence, it's a poor excuse for actual conversation.

While I do not desire to make answering my letters prove a burden to you, you know full well you cannot write too soon, too often, nor too long.

Hopefully Yours,
J.B.M

---

*JBM's mother died when he was quite young, perhaps ten years old. Why there was a strained relationship with his father, and possibly with his sister Kate, has not been explained.

Lampasas, Texas
Jan. 1, 1889

My Dear Mollie,

The first day of the new year was made very pleasant by its bringing to me this morning a long letter *from* you, and I celebrate its closing by writing *to* you . . . .

It has always been a mystery to me, since I've reached the age of letter writing, why it is that nearly every person, if they have written more than four pages, will invariably say at the close, "Well, I guess you have enough of this" when they know full well that the reader has not had enough. I must inform you right now that when the close of your letter was reached, altho' you had written eleven pages, I began at the beginning again and managed someway to "wade" thro' it a second time. Even after a second wading I wished for more, and spent some time in speculating what the twelfth page might have contained had you filled it with some of your unuttered thoughts.

With the samples I have in my possession of your letters, *I* fail to discover that you cannot do yourself credit on paper, but appreciate the fact that *you* are inclined to do yourself an injustice by not giving to your accomplishments the credit they deserve. A remark that I made seems to be on your mind considerably. I said you did not talk as much now as you did six years ago. I was far from meaning that you did not talk as *well* now, or that you talked too much then. In other words, the night I sat with you on the banks of the San Saba [River], the few short hours spent in your company two weeks ago and your two letters, the scene six years old as fresh in my memory as today's letter, all prove to me that altho' you may have changed in many respects, my "exalted opinion," which you treat sarcastically, has not altered in the slightest....

I am ever so glad that you are on "speaking" terms once more with Aunt Em and family.[1] I think so much of them myself, and they appear to think so much of me, and feeling their treatment of you more than you felt it yourself, had "bothered" me no little....

I guess you will not have to undergo the pleasure (?) of answering this. The last link in the chain binding me to Lampasas has been broken, and I will shortly take my departure for the sunny south east.[2]

So you perceive, altho' you may not be "credulous to comprehend," the fact that you are capable of changing the course of my "mad career." I hadn't the slightest idea of leaving here when I went to Austin, but I came back with the conviction fully developed that a change of some kind was imminent.

If my first letter to you had not been answered to a certain extent favorably, I should have gone anyway somewhere. It would have been impossible for me to have settled down again to enjoy the monotony surrounding this section, feeling as I should have felt.

When I told Mr. Campbell I expected to bid an affectionate farewell to *The Leader* he asked me what I expected to do. I told him my future movements depended on circumstances upon which they had never depended before. He asked if 'twas a lady. I told him it was. . . .

I will be down by special train, and if I think the roads are passable, will start Thursday. Very likely I will go by Cousin Lillie's, and if you have a standing invitation out there, give Thad a hint you will go out with him about Friday or Saturday.[3] You see I'm a great schemer. No one will know, but you, that I'm anywhere in the country, and you, of course, will be very much surprised to see me. If I do not meet you then, I will suppose you failed to give the hint, and will proceed to interview you in regard to the failure as soon as possible.

Unless "the rains descend, and the floods come" and the bottom falls out of the roads, I will see you very soon, farewell—

Yours "Sincerely"

J.B.M.

[1] Aunt Em is Emily Townsand, a sister of J.B.M.'s mother, Jane Rebecca Townsand McGill. All of these relatives are residents of Austin, and any coolness in Mollie's reception probably stemmed from no more than her being an outsider.

[2] J.B.M. is on the staff of the newspaper, the *Lampasas Leader*, owned by W.T. Campbell. Apparently he has given Mr. Campbell notice of his plans to leave since he returned from meeting Mollie in Austin.

[3] Thad is Thaddeus Constantine Bell, another cousin of Mollie's, and brother-in-law to "Cousin Lillie." Where she lives that McGill plans to visit is unknown, but no doubt is close to Austin.

NOTE: *The rains do not descend nor the floods come, and he does see her soon, but the visit apparently is a disappointing one to J.B.M.*

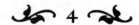

Fort Worth, Feb. 1, 1888[9]

My Little Girl,

I think this is our usual time for saying good night and although you might possibly be willing to dispense with the ceremony, I will have to inflict it upon you. I have several reasons for writing this, but one is sufficient to give, and that is I can't help it. If I'm a little more sentimental tonight than usual, consider all the circumstances and be merciful.

Don't you feel a little bit flattered and happy that you are first in the thoughts of at least one individual who, although he may feel somewhat lonely now, and when he registered at the hotel a few moments ago, had to stop and consider in what part of the world he lived, loves you more tonight than any one ever loved you before, and would exchange everything he holds most dear for just one little spark of affection from you.

I might as well have expected the earth to cease its revolutions as to think that being away could take you from my thoughts. Twenty-four hours absence, at least, has not made the situation any more endurable, and the continual talk of fellow passengers on the train today has not helped me to forget. Every farmer I saw at work in his field would remind me of the fact that if he had a wife at home who loved him, he was more of a success than myself. I saw two convict gangs at work on the Railroad, and thought that if any one had left a loving woman at home when he went to prison, while he might be an outcast from respectable society, he had gained the one thing that *I* so far have failed to gain.

It's just a month ago today since I wrote to you last. The situation has so changed that I can scarcely realize I'm the same man. I expected then to see you in a few days. My hopes were so high and my resolution so great that I could and would make you love me. If I had been told by an angel from the unknown world that after learning to care for you more than I thought I could ever care for anyone, I would in one short month be writing to you again in any way but as a successful lover, I should have been inclined to doubt the messenger.

If I could bring myself to your belief that's it's not possible for you to love, I do not think 'twould be much "satisfaction." But the thought that some other man may be able to occupy the place in your regard which I have striven so hard to occupy is almost maddening.

I'm not going to write you much tonight. 'Tis useless to repeat what you already know so well, and I cannot write in any other strain all at once. But one thing I must say, in all our conversation, whenever I've said anything to wound you in any way, consider that I did not mean it. Whatever the future may hold for either of us, together or separately as you so finally decide, remember I hold you blameless, and look on you as the one woman above all others for me, whom I love with my whole soul, and for whose happiness I will undergo everything, even to living without you. But don't force me to do this.

It was like tearing my heart out to tell you good bye last night, although I tried to keep you from knowing it. It's equally hard tonight, but I could not help it. While you might consider it a weakness in men in general to be so affectionate, you will not consider very severely one who exercises this feeling towards yourself.

Goodnight, My Dear Little Girl, Goodnight,

J.

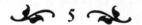

Office of H. N. Garrett,
Tax Assessor,
Martin County, Texas
Marienfeld, Texas, Feb. 5th, 1889

My Dear Mollie:

I intended not to write you again until I had received a letter *from* you, but an ever present desire to talk to you forces me to be impatient. I will make an effort, however, this time to be a little more like an iceberg than I was the other night in Fort Worth. I imagine I do not feel quite so "broken up" as I did then and can write in a little less despairing style, but I don't know that I have any desire to unwrite that letter. I think I felt about as "blue" then as a person ever feels. I found myself comparing two departures from Austin, and the nights following, nearly ten years apart.

I left home the first time horseback, with possibly ten dollars capital. The night after leaving I slept on the ground with my saddle for a pillow. While gazing at the stars, I looked the future in the face, and was somewhat impressed with the idea that my prospects might have been more flattering, but I do not remember feeling particularly disheartened. Friday night, although in a comfortable room in a hotel with a slightly increased capital, I think would have been willingly exchanged for the one spent on the prairie when I thought the future comparatively bright.

On reaching here, I realized the truth of the scriptural quotation, "A prophet is not without honor, save in his own country." Out here where the inhabitants to a considerable extent look out for "number one," and are not much given to affection, to be met on every side with hands extended in greeting and to *feel* that their owners were glad to see you again makes one think he *may* be worth liking, even if his girl *does* fail to love him a little.

Notwithstanding all this, I find myself now indulging in contrasts and wonder how for several years I not only endured the life I lived here, but was to some extent contented and happy while living it. Sunday afternoon, I was in a sitting room with four ladies, three married and one single, and thought, while listening to their conversation, that what I told you about living two different lives was more clearly demonstrated than I had before realized. The contrast was so great between the woman I had in my mind as a model and themselves, that I almost wondered if my life the past month had been real and not a dream. It may be a dream in one sense, that is, something that will never come to pass, but is one that has so lifted me out of the past, that wishing for its realization will not render the future for me very "satisfactory."

I find law suits not much better calculated to afford gratification to one's desires than love suits, but I also discover that the former hasn't the power over one's thoughts that the latter possesses. My case was the first on the docket Monday morning, but owing to some carelessness on the other side their evidence was not ready and the suit was continued until next term of court.

The other cases similar to mine were tried and settled favorably to the boys here.*. . .

If my absence has caused any change in your attitude, and you discover that having me with you continually is a thought that is not very disagreeable, you will make me exceedingly happy. On the other hand, if you find my absence is preferable to my presence, while it will hurt me as much now as ever to hear it, I will endeavor not to ''abuse'' you as I did on a former occasion.

My attitude is unchangeable, and until you give yourself to some other fellow I shall call you mine. I consider you worth any amount of time I devote to your capture. The longer it takes, the more determined I shall become, because I dislike to waste my energies. I think if you realized what a perservering individual with whom you had to contend, as possibly you may have heard me remark, you would submit to the inevitable.

I will know better after receiving one or two letters from you how to write. I am laboring to some extent in the dark, the only light by which I can guide myself being my love for you.

I don't think of any excuse you can give for not writing me often and long, except feeling it a bore. If such be the case, don't do it. Otherwise I will expect you to help brighten an existence which, since knowing you, is not as contented as it was before.

Faithfully Yours
J.B.M.

---

*Civil Case #4 in Martin County is recorded as the Western Wool Commission Company of St. Louis, Missouri, vs. John Barclay McGill. A half dozen other identical suits were filed by the commission company at the same time, suing each of several wool growers for a balance due. Apparently the wool had been turned over to the company on consignment; the company estimated the price that could be realized and paid the grower an advance. In the suit, the company contended that the market had declined and too much money had been advanced. The jurors were sheepmen themselves; the cases were decided against the St. Louis firm. JBM's case, filed in August 1888, was dismissed finally in November 1889.

Miss Mollie McCormick
908 San Antonio St.
Austin, Texas
    (Forwarded to Graham, Young Co.)

Marienfeld, Feb.13, 1889

My Dear Mollie,
    I'm writing this under a sense of disappointment so keen as to be almost unendurable, but I will try not to bore you. I have written you twice, once from Fort Worth the night after leaving Austin, and once since coming here. I've waited in vain for a reply. I cannot think that you have received them and not answered, without some good reason. I believe your own sense of justice would compel you to write me, if only a few lines. I would like to ask you if either or both of the letters were received, and whether you have written?
    Please be perfectly candid. I do not think I can suffer, mentally, any worse than I have suffered during the last thirteen days.
    I would like to look forward to the time when I should see you again, but if I have to add to my disappointment, the fact that you were glad to be rid of me, I think I can be generous enough not to trouble you again. If my presence proved disagreeable, I regret it, but do not think 'twas altogether my fault. You remember you told me it was not often a woman objected to being loved.
    Don't let fear that you may raise false hopes prevent your writing to me. I will take your letters just as they are meant, and be glad to get them.
    I must ask again as a matter of justice that you reply to this at once. I think you owe me this much. I have tried to keep myself under control while writing this, but it's terribly hard to refrain from saying "I love you" on every line.
    Very often it has been the case that letters have been lost, and because the individuals at either end of the line were too proud to write without answers, life-time mistakes have been made. I will not believe,

until you tell me, that you have received mine and have not replied.

It has been all I could do several times to keep from resolving to go to Austin again, but knowing 'twould be a weakness for which you would feel the utmost contempt has prevented the resolution being taken.

Good-bye
Unchangeably yours.
J.B.M.

My address is Marienfeld, Martin Co.*

---

*Martin County is in far West Texas, just west of Big Spring. In about 1890, the town's name was changed from Marienfeld to Stanton, the present-day county seat.

7

Marienfeld, Feb. 23/89

My Dear Mollie,

I was glad to discover upon reading your letter that your reason for not writing sooner was one that I can understand. I had been endeavoring for some time to think if there was anything which would excuse you, and have worried over it so much that I went to the telegraph office two or three days ago and sent a message to Mr. Andrews, asking him two or three questions, and one was, if you were still in Austin.[1] It helped me considerably when he answered you were gone.

If I had not acted on your theory in writing this, that second thoughts are better than first thoughts, very likely I should have sent off a missive that would have put you in a bad humor, and been regretted by myself as a falsehood long before it reached its destination. After mature deliberation, I hope I can keep myself from being very disagreeable.

After this letter, I will try to conform as near as possible to your wishes, that our correspondence shall be confined strictly to friendly letters. If I over-step the bounds occasionally, you must be lenient. The few short days and the fore-parts of the nights forming the month of January, 1889, cannot be blotted from my memory so quickly nor completely as the chilly and indifferent tone of your letter would indicate they had been blotted from yours. Although I understood then almost as well as now, that I would be the worst sufferer when we said good-bye.

Nevertheless, if you had said anything in your letter leading me to believe that my presence in Austin had added anything to your pleasure, and that you missed me in the slightest, 'twould have made me feel better. I will not complain any more now, and as I said, after this letter you will not be "pestered" much with sentiment.

I think I also said, in talking of seeing you again, that I should prefer to wait until I could meet you on equal grounds. Whether that time will be next spring or next summer, I cannot say. I do not care to live over the last three weeks again. While I think I can stand your letters, if they are all as *Cousinly* as the one just received, without being "hopelessly wrecked," I do not think I can very soon place myself within range of a pair of the most talkative and love inspiring eyes into which a man ever looked, and completely lost his heart by looking.

When a woman surrounds herself with an impenetrable wall of ice, and a fellow gets as badly hurt as I have been in trying to gain access to her affection, if he ever does recover his balance he will try to think of some other mode of attack and will be very careful, should he sustain a second defeat that the consequences will not be so lasting. Such is my case, and while I've tried to be as unselfish in my wishes as I imagine a man ever is, I should like to have my affections under better control before I take my chances of being a second time "wrecked on the rocks of your indifference."

I've thought of this expression hundreds of times since I first used it; but never imagined at that time what effect such a wreck could have on me. This is not following your wishes of a friendly correspondence very closely, is it? But what I would like to impress on you, if you are not already impressed, is this, that should I in the future, forbear from treading on forbidden ground, you will understand 'tis in compliance with your desire and not that I have forgotten.

Right here I want you to make me two promises. I don't think you have made me any before. One is that you will not give yourself to any other fellow solely because you think you are necessary to his happiness. I think I have a prior claim on this point. The other is that you will not *try* to care for anyone else, but your endeavors will be against such a feeling. I hope you will do me the justice to think I deserve two such promises, and that you will consider them if made, more sacred than such promises usually are.

I have enjoyed (?) only one dissipation since I've been here. Thursday night I went out to a dance twenty miles west of here, given in honor of two young married couples. 'Twas a rough crowd. I had never met any of the young ladies before, and shall not regret it much if I never see any of them again. They were putting on quite a lot of style, having printed programs. I was introduced to one and borrowed her card and looked it over. Very few of the dances were filled, but after taking a good look at her, I handed the program back saying I was very sorry, but she had no dances left that I could go thro' with.

In a little while some man gave me an introduction to another, and the same process was repeated, except I put my name down for a quadrille towards the bottom of the list. When I thought 'twas our time I went after her, and was informed that the quadrille for which I was entered was "done danced." I don't think my regrets for being late were very sincere.

I had quite a long letter from Janie a few days ago in reply to one written her shortly after I left Austin.[2] I was feeling that my joke on her in regard to what she said to Thad and me was a little hard, and wrote her that I hoped 'twould not be entered against me. Among other things she said Mr. Spence had taken up with, or was trying to do so, with Mary again. That young man has my sincerest sympathy, or I might say I envy him. It seems to make very little difference how he is treated by one girl, he has several more to fall back upon.

If he is hurt by each one as badly as I have been *once*, I cannot find it in my heart to condemn him for trying to end his fickle career by the intemperate use of hard boiled eggs.[3]

I have the same excuse for saying good-night that you had, it's nearly train time. Please write me soon. I shall not be in Marienfeld, I think, many days longer at present. I expect to be on the move nearly altogether for the next few months, but this will be my post office for a while. I would like to hear from you again before I leave.

Remember me to Cousin Sallie and other relations.[4]

Faithfully,
J.B. McGill

[1] Mr. Andrews is a cousin by marriage.

[2] Janie is J.B.M.'s first cousin, Aunt Em's daughter.

[3] The danger in hard boiled eggs remains a mystery. Did he eat too many and make himself sick? Did he try to swallow one whole? The facts are lost.

[4] Cousin Sallie is Mollie's sister, two years older.

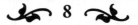

Marienfeld, March 8/89

My Dear Mollie,

Shortly after writing you last, I had an invitation from a friend to go on a trip with him to the country above here, and consequently my uncertain movements began somewhat earlier than I thought when I wrote you.

I returned last night after a ten days absence and found your letter awaiting me. I was in a very pleasant frame of mind anyway, and after reading your letter I was still more so.

I have been observing life under adverse circumstances while I was away, adverse both as regards the observer and the observed. I hardly know whether I have arrived at any definite conclusions or not.

The furtherest point of our journey was more than one hundred miles from a post office, and we collected quite a number of letters to be mailed on our return. The days of the week and month were items the people did not try to keep up with. Visitors from the railroad were hailed with delight so we were very hospitably treated wherever we stopped. With few exceptions both men and women were laboring under a chronic complaint of discontent, and the principal subject of their conversation was abuse of the country.

Strange to say, the happiest and most perfectly satisfied man whom I met was one for whose life and surroundings all his neighbors on either side expressed their sympathy. We ate dinner at his ranch one day. He was on the down hill side of life, over fifty years old I should guess, and living out in the middle of a desert almost entirely alone, riding out after his cattle in every kind of weather that Texas can produce. Yet one would have to search long and closely to find a man who was more supremely contented with his lot than was this one. Still, as I said before, all his neighbors not having enough to do to complain for themselves, found time to pity *him*. It strikes me that such characters are rather to be envied.

I stopped at a ranch one night, and was very cordially greeted by an individual whom I failed to recognize. He appeared to know me so well that I was ashamed to ask him who he was, and puzzled my brain some time to try to remember him. Finally, he asked me when I'd been in Austin last, and how Mary and Janie were, calling them by their first names.

I suppose I answered his questions all right, but to hear those two names spoken in familiar tones by a rough looking cowboy in the middle of the "staked plains" had a kind of stupefying effect on me. After recovering from the shock, I asked one of the other fellows around the house, who that person might be. It turned out to be Ed Roesler, a brother of Miss Josephine, and I guess 'twas only natural he should inquire after the welfare of his first cousins. The last time I saw him was in '82, and he has grown so that 'twas not strange I should not have known him.

After long and careful speculation on the subject, both from personal experience and observations of others, I think I can venture a timid conclusion. That is, temporary physical discomfort is preferable to prolonged mental disquietude.

These people have comparatively comfortable houses, plenty to eat, and are moderately well off financially. In winter during bad weather, they have a rough time, but it does not last long. People in the east of the same class, or even several degrees higher in society, are continually worried about thousands of things of which these in the west know nothing.

My companion and myself started out one evening from one ranch to go to another twelve miles away across the prairie, without any road. A cold north east wind was blowing, and the clouds were helping to make things more disagreeable. As a natural result of all these combinations, we were soon rather damp, cold, and lost, but luckily managed to find our way to the place we started for soon after dark.

There were nine men, including ourselves, in a room about twelve feet square, all trying to get warm by a cooking stove, which the owner of the ranch had ironically named the "refrigerator." After a warm supper, however, we spread our blankets on the floor and were soon perfectly comfortable, feeling much more so, probably, on account of hearing the wind outside. I think this one night would have convinced me that my conclusion regarding physical discomfort is right.

I received a telegram from Thad this morning informing me that the great event which he and Miss F. had been anticipating for four years would come off on the twelfth of this month, and requesting my presence.* I thought on it some time and have finally decided that while this country out here is rather lonesome, Austin without you would be more so. I guess I shall send my "regrets" through the mail.

I guess they must have "set the day" rather suddenly, because I had a *letter* from T. last night written a few days ago, and he did not mention the subject. Well, I'm glad they are going to be made happy at last. The saying is that "all things come to the man who waits," but I'm inclined to think there are frequent exceptions, and waiting is sometimes rather hard to do.

I guess my wanderings will be confined to Texas and possibly its next door neighbor, New Mexico. The line between them is imaginary. I've about made my mind to drift back again, for the present at least, to my old pursuit, and put into practice again my theory mentioned about discomforts. I have no idea how long I can compel myself to be satisfied. Not a great while I expect, but as long as I can look forward to the time when you and I are going to try to make each other happy, I may be able to work for both of us.

I *did* intend to write this letter without any remarks whatever of the preceding character, but I think I've done remarkably well as it is, considering the length of this epistle.

I expect to go away again in a few days and do not know exactly when I shall return. Any time within the next ten days or two weeks that you feel in a communicative mood, if you will sit down and write me your "observations and conclusions" and have it here to welcome me on my return, you will, if such a thing be possible, which it is not, bind me still closer to you.

I trust that in the foregoing I have not trespassed too much on forbidden ground to displease. I have some hopes that in the course of time I may be able to commence my letters "Dear Cousin," and close them in like style. If I should, remember it is only to comply with your tastes, and do not imagine for a moment that "the villain is resting from the pursuit."

Yours affectionately,
J.B. McGill

* Thad C. Bell is to marry Miss Florence Whitis on March 12, 1889.

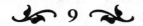

Marienfeld, March 29/89

My Dear Mollie,

I returned to M. several days ago, and have been abusing myself continually, because I had instructed you to wait two weeks before writing. I must express my thanks to you that you did not make me wait any longer for a letter. I wish I could invent some collection of words that would convey to you some idea of how much I appreciate hearing from you, but if I were to try, I expect you would think, "Well, he is the 'softest' individual I ever met." Without exaggeration, however, and without *much* softness, I can say that I do not expect you ever did or ever will write any letters that will cause the recipients as much happiness as those you write to me.

I haven't heard from Austin since Thad's wedding, and did not know of his wedding tour to Mexico. Whether he combined business with pleasure, I cannot say, but unless he did, I think a "honey-moon" anywhere in his case, was bowing down and worshiping the customs of society more than sober judgment would allow.

I do not think it probable that he has secured any office, because I have been watching the recent appointments rather closely, and have seen none that would benefit him. He wrote me that he had sold his horses, and I guess he is speculating in railroads at the rate of three cents per mile on this raise.

I don't mean the above as sarcasm, but I think a little economy under certain circumstances should be practiced, (by others, I mean, I don't know how myself.) When Dr. Wright was married, the Austin folks were situated, financially, about as they are now. Still, a wedding and supper, costing several hundred dollars was thought necessary for the momentous occasion.[1]

If I can't fill up my letters describing scenes *away* from Marienfeld, I'm afraid my communications *would* require a stretch of your imagination to make them appear interesting, because while the six or eight young fellows of us forming the "society" of this city, are great on building "air-castles," we seldom carry any scheme into execution that is worthy of note.

During my last excursion I confined myself to the settled portion of the country and did not go off the R.R.s. I was two or three days in Cisco, and my thoughts very frequently wandered away towards the north. I wondered what you would think if I were to give way to the temptation, and traverse the sixty miles which separated . . .

I went to church twice, giving each of yours a trial, the Methodist and the Southern or Democratic Presbyterian. I listened to the Methodist minister with a great deal of interest, but for originality the sermon was somewhat lacking. I think he came nearer making his discourse out of anecdotes, weaving them together in a connected shape, than anyone I ever heard.

The Democratic Presbyterian minister at Abilene, I did not like so well. I met him after church, and he seemed to say "As I happen to be a preacher I suppose I must talk to you." As you and I have the same presentiments on a *very few* things, I think the same thought would likely come over us in this case, which would be this. "As I have been raised to treat men of your calling with politeness I suppose I will have to listen to you."

While in Abilene I spent most of the time with Dr. Stiles, and found him more sociable than he has the reputation of being in his native town.[2] We discussed nearly everything and everybody either of us knew. I did not grow confidential, however. Consequently, my last trip to Austin was not discoursed upon very largely.

I found him not much more in love with the people there, than they were with him. He informed me that Mr. James Downie had passed through not long ago on his way to the Capital City, and that he had his wedding "outfit" with him, although no time had been agreed upon for the ceremony. He was taking his clothes along so as to be ready in a case of emergency. I suppose he intends to "camp" near his girl until she is ready to go back with him.

From your description of the Graham escorts, I would infer that the young gentleman known to history as the one who "would his quietus make" with hard boiled eggs, would rank among them as captain. I wish you would inform me if Col. Crawford is married, or possibly you had better let me think that he is, and not tell me otherwise. I feel far enough off now, and if I had the fact before me, that an unencumbered man had made such an impression on you in one afternoon, as he seems to have made, I can't think how I should endure it.

I think your remark in regard to its being distasteful to me to be reminded of the fact that we are cousins, is rather unkind, if you intended to be sarcastic. . . .

As far as *you* are concerned, until a few months ago, I took the same pride in being a cousin of yours as I do now in bearing that relation to your sisters. Since a certain date of which you are well aware, I learned to think so much of you, that cousinly regard entirely disappeared. . . .

But I'm thankful to say for this reason only, and you *know* its the only one, that the connection is so distant, the most vivid imagination could not offer it as a bar. Consequently, so far as you and I are concerned, My *Dear* Cousin, to be reminded of the fact that your Grand Father and my Grand Mother were brother and sister neither adds to my felicity nor takes from it.

You can gather as a deduction from the foregoing that I feel myself at liberty to erase from the address of your letters the title of relationship, and you have the same privilege in regard to interlining address on mine.

I will not place any restrictions on your time, in answering this. I will be waiting for your letter when it comes. I wish I could know that you get as much "satisfaction" out of writing to me as I do from writing to you. Such knowledge as this *would* add to my felicity.

Yours affectionately,
J.B. McGill

[1] Dr. Edward B. Wright, pastor of the First Presbyterian Church in Austin for forty years, had married Thad's sister, Evelyn Hunter Bell.

[2] Dr. Edmond P. Stiles was another brother-in-law of Thad's, being married to Lucy Copes Bell. For obscure reasons, he was not well-liked by the "Family."

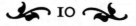

10

Marienfeld April 10, 1889

My Dear Mollie,
Like a ray of sunlight showing itself through the clouds on a dismal day, your letters come, and help to break the monotony of a somewhat

dismal existence, not exactly dismal possibly, but certainly not crowded with variety. I'm not feeling unusually brilliant tonight, and if this epistle proves very doleful 'twill be quite natural. Strange to say, too, the dolefulness will arise from physical causes and not *mental*, as some of my forlorn letters to you heretofore have been caused.

For several days I've been afflicted with a complaint very rarely heard of in Texas, namely a "bad cold;" but I think now I have it under control. The remedy I used is very simple, but I trust effective. I went to town this afternoon (I've been sojourning in the country a few days). Making myself conspicuous with an overwhelming desire to cough, and frequently yielding to the desire, I was presented with a small package of herbs gathered in some distant part of the earth known as. . . . I'm afraid to try to spell it but the pronunciation is "hoar-hound."

I was presented along with the herbs, with full verbal directions, but do not think I entirely carried them out. Something was said about making candy, but if the viand I concocted, and the remains of which is now before me is *candy*, then you and I were grossly imposed upon last winter when we patronized the Austin factories.

My "modus operandi" was as follows. I placed on the stove a small kettle with a cup of water in it. I then put into this possibly two cups of sugar. When the sugar had dissolved, I very carefully deposited some of the herbs. I suppose it cooked for thirty minutes, and I then poured the mixture into a plate well greased for the purpose. After the heat had departed from this chaotic mass and it had cooled down to a solid, its hardness was almost equal to Italian marble, and its surface presented the same appearance as would the Atlantic Ocean if that body of water should suddenly freeze during one of its most violent storms. I had my doubts about it, but as Mr. Billings said about "hash," "I eat it and still live."

I feel very proud of the foregoing pages. I had no idea I could make the doleful part of this letter so lengthy.

I've been reading lately the book that so many critics are exercising their minds over, *Robert Elsmere*. As I do not set up for a critic I will not inflict upon you my opinions on the book, but there are some things in there which bear very strongly on my own individual case in the matters of beliefs and disbeliefs concerning religion. I do not know whether or not you have read the book, but trust I can make myself plain if you have not.

Robert Elsmere is a rector of some Church of England church, a very sincere and enthusiastic man. He is a great historical and scientific reader and becomes acquainted with several very learned men. History, science, and the knowledge of these men combined cause him to begin to have doubts concerning the divine origin of the New Testament. His struggles *against* his doubts for months are very vividly portrayed. He uses every means known to him to set them aside and go back to the point where he was, before he began to *reason*. But finally, being too conscientious to stand in a church Sunday after Sunday and try to make people believe what he did not believe himself, he resigns his charge and withdraws from the ministry, almost breaking the heart of his wife, a very zealous churchwoman to whom he is devotedly attached, and raising up a wall between himself and her which was never completely obliterated during his life.*

Now for the personal application. I'm no great historical nor scientific reader, nor have I any familiar intercourse with very learned men. But I have my doubts all the same, different very likely in many instances from the hero of this book, but which I'd like just as well as he to have removed, and which the more I try to *reason* out the more confirmed they become. As he says once, why was a man gifted with the power to think if 'twas not intended that he *should* think?

I have no doubt but there are thousands of people situated just as Robert Elsmere was or just as I am.

Now the question arises, which in my mind caused the most serious doubt of all as to the truth and teachings of the Christian religion. Why is it that we have these arguments in our minds or with each other? To make the number moderate I think I can say one fourth of the people in whose minds they arise, decide in favor of reason and against religion. The majority of these so deciding are people who would prefer by far to *know* that the principals [sic] they had been taught from infancy, and the principals [sic] under which their forefathers for generations back had lived and died, were infallibly and unalterably true.

Don't imagine that I get my ideas and doubts from the works of skeptical authors. Their books are my pet aversion and I prefer reading a "dime novel" on Indian fighting to one of the essays from their pens.

I expect my letters to you will be something like Cousin Tom Campbell said of his brother James's. Cousin Jim was supposed to write a letter to his girl every Sunday afternoon, I think. If I were to look over the list of all my acquaintances, either relations or otherwise, I believe I should choose Jim Campbell as the man with the least sentiment. Tom said he knew Jim confined himself strictly to business in those letters until he reached the last two or three lines and then possibly put in an affectionate word or two. I will do a little better than this, however, and will devote a *page* or two to your edification and enlightenment on this question.

I never thought that I understood woman's ways remarkably well, but you are one too many for me. It seems that you don't think I care enough for you to go sixty miles to see you. Then you think all I said to you in person, and all I wrote before you placed such prohibitory injunctions on me, was not meant.

Well, I *know* you don't think anything of the kind. *You* know whenever you'll give me the least sign in the world that my love for you makes any more impression than it did two months ago, that if I had to start from this point and travel in a *westwardly* course until I reached you the distance in miles would not be considered.

But I'll inform you, My Little Girl, what hurts and it *hurts bad*. When a fellow is standing up by the side of a woman he loves better than he does his life, lays one arm over her shoulders, and endeavors to draw her to him, and he feels her shrinking, no matter however so slightly, from his touch, he feels there is a greater distance between himself and her than a mere question of miles. I can't stand it a second time just yet.

You are as dear to me today as you ever were, and only I realize how dear that is, but the knowledge of the fact that you do not love me just a *little* bit is easier to submit to away from the sound of your voice, and out of the reach of a glance from your eyes, than it would be nearer.

I don't know whether there is any hidden meaning in your remark about Mr. Downie's being a sensible young man or not. If you think 'twould be a good place for me to follow his example, and camp near you until you came to terms, I wish you would say so. Don't take offense now and say you never intended it for a hint, because if I had thought so I would have been looking for a good camping place before this letter reaches you. If you can put up with my letters, I will try to put up with yours, so we will agree not to apologize.

"If you love me as I love you," you will write very soon.

Yours Affectionately,
J.B. McGill

* Gertrude Himmelfarb, an analyst of the Victorian Age in England with which the present account is contemporary, discusses the ascendency of religious doubt in the period, and relates it to Victorian morality. "Feeling guilty about the loss of their religious faith . . . [the Victorians] were determined to make of morality a substitute of religion— to make of it, indeed, a form of religion." *Marriage and Morals Among the Victorians.* (New York: Random House, 1987).

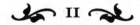 II

Marienfeld Apr. 29/89

My Dear Mollie,

I suppose you will be thinking that what I said to you once, about never seeing the girl that I cared to write to long, is beginning to effect me with you, but to use your words, such inference is wrong. My only excuse is simply selfishness. When I mail a letter to you I begin to count the days before I can possibly receive a reply, and then all kinds of speculations puzzle my brain until I *do* receive one, if you happen to be a few hours slow in answering. . . .

I'm still sojourning in the country, but not because Marienfeld is too lively, rather because the country is the more animated place at this season of the year. Nearly all the inhabitants are on their ranches, and to be in a *town* where there are no people is more lonely than in the country where you do not expect them.

I have another invitation to a ball at Midland this week, but do not think I shall attend. The one two months ago was bad enough, but *this* invitation reads "Masquerade ball," and Midland society is too much for me when you can see its face. It *should* be disguised, but I prefer the quiet of the country, if I *am* wedded to city life. I wonder what you'll have me wedded to next.

I don't know but what I should like to live in a city, though, if everything was favorable, financially I mean. I have always liked to be among the crowd at the top, and there's never a time when you cannot find yourself a resting place in some locality in the neighborhood of this enviable position.

I sometimes think that, rather than be numbered with the struggling masses at the bottom, or even in the middle, I should prefer living with one or two congenial spirits (I was about to say alone) in the center of some isolated spot, where we would be "monarchs of all we surveyed" even if our range of vision did not look over much that was valuable. With these sentiments, and a very poor prospect of getting to the top in a metropolis, my chances of living in a city, you see, are somewhat limited.

You were wrong, I think, in imagining that I would say you did not know what you were talking about in your advice regarding religion, but if you have any antidote against *thinking*, either on this subject or any other, you'd do me the greatest favor to make it known. I'm not trying to get up a religious *argument* with you, because we are both virtually on the same side and I trust not a great way apart. I expect my worst trouble is as Dr. Wright once said to me, that my fear of being considered in the slightest hypocritical, would prevent my saying I believed things that I could possibly have any doubt about.

Most people who try to make their own doubts excuses for non acceptance of Christianity, I know do it because it suits their convenience and lives better to disbelieve, but I don't think this has ever influenced me. Even if it had in the past, I don't think a man ever needed something to look forward to more than I do now. My past existence has not been overflowing with seriousness of any kind, but I think the last few monotonous years must have exhausted my stock of cheerfulness completely.

I've been vainly endeavoring, since I told you good bye three months ago, to imagine what the remainder of this life would be without you. While you may find it hard to believe that such is the case, twenty-four hours of it would be more than I'd be particularly anxious to go through with.

I expect I'd better stop. I know you are very much shocked now, and I know too that I am violating our contract whenever I depart from mere friendliness. But I'd like to number the man among my acquaintances who could write to the woman he loves without telling her so.

Remember me to your family,

Affectionately Yours,
J.B. McGill

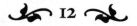 12

Marienfeld May 7, 1889

My Dear Mollie,

Did the idea ever occur to you that I am a very remarkable individual? I am very much impressed with that sentiment myself at the present moment, in this regard. The more deplorable and disagreeable the surroundings, the higher my spirits soar. I feel on the top round of the ladder of light-heartedness tonight.

The surroundings are as follows. Camped out on the "lone prairie," miles away from anywhere, with no other company than one of the representatives of the ancient order of Aztecs commonly called a Mexican. My only light is produced by a continual application of small sticks to a bed of coals, but you have seen me build fires for heating purposes, and the appearance of this will convience you that I am also a proficient in the art of building them for light.

I have a fair prospect of sitting up several hours and concluded to inflict on you some of my nonsense. I am moving a flock of the subjects of tariff legislation out to the ranch, and a sheep has, among other admirable qualities, an inordinate love for moonlight, positively refusing to retire before that luminary sinks to rest. The moon is now some distance above the horizon, consequently my bed-time is not yet.

Then I had still another reason for writing to you. I knew if I waited until I reached Marienfeld before answering your letter, that I hope is waiting for me, you would be very uneasy about me and possibly worry yourself sick, so I thought it would be best to relive your mind by writing on the road.

If you don't think 'twould be "crowd'n' the mourners," I would appreciate another letter from you when I get home, taking it for granted that you have already written once since I left. You may give this any name you like. Some man once said, it did not make so much difference *how* you read as *what* you read. I suppose the saying will hold good in writing and in that case, I think I have done myself credit.

I haven't any envelope, nor stamps, and a fastidious person might think I was not *very* well "fixed" for ink and paper.* I am also several miles from a post office, but fortunately I have a friend who is operator at a little telegraph office which I pass tomorrow, and I think I can make use of him to get this forwarded to its destination.

Please write to me again, won't you, Little Girl, about this time next week?

Yours affectionately,
J.B.M.

* This letter is written in pencil on ledger paper, and the post mark seems to read "Texas & El Paso R.P.O. W.D."

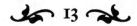

13

Marienfeld May 19th 1889

My Dear Mollie,

Unless you received a letter I wrote you several days ago, I guess 'twill be almost useless for me to try to convince you this time that my delay in writing to you was not my fault. But I *did* write you a missive nearly two weeks ago, informing you of the fact that I was wandering in the wilds some distance from this point, and would not get your letter as soon as you might think. Whether this epistle reached you or not I'm unable to say, but think it a matter of doubt. I placed it in the hands of a telegraph operator on the R.R. and asked him if he would mail it without fail. He said if he mailed it at all, 'twould be without failing, and with this unsatisfactory reply, I was forced to be content. . . .

Whatever your traits of character may be that I have *not* learned, I know enough to realize that if you will let me combine all the adjectives describing them into one little word, I will say you are the "nicest" little girl I ever knew, and the only one I ever cared to possess. Or ever will care to, I expect.

Two great events have taken place here within the last two days. Yesterday, Marienfeld turned out in a body and had a picnic, and today we had preaching in English (we have it in German every Sunday). I think I acted very generously on the picnic question. I loaned my buggy out to a couple of ladies, and drove a wagon-load of children out to the grounds. I do not claim any credit, however, for this piece of self-denial, because I had more satisfaction out of the children than I could any other way.

I believe *one* unmarried lady was the only individual of this description on the ground, and her presence did not add to the attractiveness of the occasion to any extent. She hailed from California, and her principal topic of conversation was contrasting the size of the trees in that state with these here, our only shade within twenty miles being formed by a small knot of trees scarcely higher than a man's head. We had a nice

Marienfeld, circa 1884–85. Courtesy Martin County Museum, Stanton, Texas.

dinner, and I put in the day very pleasantly, nothwithstanding the absence of young ladies. I "stand in" pretty well with all the married ladies, and two or three times during the day when talking to a group of these, I would have the advice thrust on me to get married. I could say more truthfully than fellows generally can that I couldn't. The answer would be, they guessed I hadn't tried very hard.

I suppose you will agree with me that their guesses were wrong, but I gather this consolation, my outside appearance and every day behavior does not betray to casual observers the conflict continuously going on within.

I went to church last night, but did not go today. I believe its better for me not to go when I have to think more about keeping awake than I do about the sermon. The preacher may have been a good man, but he was an exquisitely poor talker. He has been camped near town for several days, with his herds and his flocks, consisting of a few cattle and horses and many children.

He was asked by someone, discovering him to be a preacher, to hold services while he was here, but such men as he, whether they be sincere or otherwise, certainly do not help along any the cause of religion. The majority of the inhabitants of Western Texas are men of possibly a little more than average intelligence. They are nearly all of them without any religion whatever, and it requires a better talker than the one here today to make them think seriously about anything.

I'm sorry for Miss Brandt's sake that she hasn't the honor of my acquaintance. Her father, or I suppose her father, is quite well known through this section of country. He is a land agent engaged in the occupation of what we call out here "hunting for suckers." A sucker is one of a class of human beings, raised somewhere in the east, supposed to have plenty of money and willing to part with it. I never heard of his having a grown daughter, but that the young lady's name does not appear on the list of the Midland Belles is more to her credit than otherwise.

Do you hear often from Austin? I suppose the fault is mine principally, but *I* never hear a word. I'm getting pretty well weaned by this time from the "scenes of my childhood," but I guess a man seldom gets so entirely over the feeling of affection for his family and friends, but that a word of news now and then concerning their welfare would be welcome.

I shall expect an early reply to this, because you've had lots of time since writing last. I appreciate your letters very much, even tho', as you say, you do not write exactly the kind I would like to have you.

Yours Affectionately,
J.B. McGill

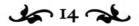

14

Marienfeld May 22/89

My Dear Mollie,

If there had been the slightest doubt in my mind the other day, when I said you were the nicest little girl I ever knew, about the truth of the assertion, these doubts would have melted away this afternoon when I received your last letter, for you certainly *are*. It doesn't always require adverse circumstances to raise my spirits, for a nice long letter from you couldn't well be construed as an item of adversity, and I feel pretty fairly tonight. If I let my imagination soar up among the clouds, don't think again that I've made a mistake in directing this letter.

I deny the charge that I ever "adorned the *editorial* staff of *The Leader*," although sometimes when the columns of that paper were likely to come from the press looking the same as when they went in, owing to a lack of reading material, I would condescend (!) to help out the editor. My farewell address was written from Austin, which I believe you enjoyed the privilege of reading.

The spirit I had with me when I wrote you that essay by the light of the campfire was not very congenial. The English language conveyed very little meaning to his Castilian intellect, and I am by no means a proficient in Spanish. Consequently, we could not hold sweet converse in a poetic strain, and let our thoughts rise in harmony above the things of earth, but were compelled to "go very slow.". . .

I think I exhausted the stock of Marienfeld news items in my last letter, so if this was intended for the local column of a newspaper, I'm afraid 'twould be deficient. We had quite a nice rain one or two nights ago. *This* is something worth recording from a region so seldom visited by showers as the staked plain. Fortunately, however, we out here are not so dependent on regular rains, as our less favored brethren in the east.

I rather expect you will have to make an exception in my favor regarding your theory of a man's not being of the same mind for three months. According to my way of reckoning time, its been one or two days over five months since I wrote you my first letter and if I know myself at all, I haven't changed much where you are concerned.

I passed a resolution to myself when I told you good-bye, that unless I could gather from your letters the impression that you thought more of me than you were willing to admit personally, and would some day consent to be my *own* little girl, only one of two considerations would ever induce me willingly to see you again. I have failed to gather any such impression, and the two considerations were, first, that I could be able to see you again any number of times, and could tell you good-bye with as little regret as I could any other girl of my acquaintance. If this had happened 'twould not have been very flattering to you and your theory in regard to a man's mind would have been strengthened.

The other consideration was that I *couldn't* stay away. I think you can flatter yourself that this last is the one that will bring me back. I never wanted to see anyone so much in my life. If the term homesick could be applied to such a feeling, then I certainly am most awfully homesick. As I have generally given way to any desire so strong as this, very likely my course will be mapped out towards Graham within the next six weeks. Of course I can come nearly any time, but I have a great faculty for *remaining* in agreeable localities and if I come to see you before the first of July or about that time, my stay would be limited. Consequently, I think 'twould be better to wait until I can come "and stay awhile."

If this reaches you before you write, you will owe me two letters in one, but I expect the two letters separate would be longer. I oughtn't to have written this so soon, but the deed is done.

Yours Affectionately,
J.B.M.

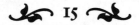 15

Marienfeld May 28/89

My Dear Mollie,

I am feeling in rather an affectionate mood tonight, and would much rather be within speaking distance of you, than to confine myself to a "cold-blooded" letter. I do not mean for you to infer that my affectionate spells only come on at intervals, because I know not the time for several months when they were absent, but there are times when it seems that my whole existence almost centered in you. I should say I was serious in this, and wanted you to think I was, if serious means in this instance being truthful. . . .

I've been fighting against my feeling for you, for months. It grows with opposition, and tonight if possible, you are dearer than you were *last* night. Yes, Little Girl, I *am* serious, and if want of experience has had anything to do with the present situation of affairs, then I'm willing to admit, 'tis a drawback.

I expect this talk of mine grows monotonous to you, but I can't help it. I asked you once, if you knew of anything you could do or say that would make me think any less of you, to do it or say it. You refused. Consequently, when I feel drawn towards you by some influence that I can no more resist than I can explain, you are in some measure, tho' possibly not wholly, responsible. If such letters as this worry you, in your next to me, you will have your revenge.

It's a curious fact, very likely unknown to you, that when I write you a letter more affectionate than usual, while reading it, I suppose, you gradually withdraw within that wall of ice, which you say my imagination has created. Your reply will be sent forth so chilling in its nature as to make me wish I had written about anything else in the world than love.

The last few times I've written to you I endeavored to keep off this topic as much as possible, and the consequence was I've had some of the nicest letters lately you've ever written me, and received them closer together. Now I'm afraid I've spoiled it all by not being able to control myself any longer, and your answer to this will be delayed several days. When it does come, 'twill make me wonder what causes such a difference in the temperature between here and Graham.

I do not know what the trouble might be between Andrew and Mary.* Any question propounded to me in regard to the differences between a fellow and his girl is "too hard." I feel confident of one thing. If the situation puzzles Andrew as much as mine puzzles me, the amount of studying he does on any other subject will not give him the headache.

I had a long letter from Mr. Campbell at Lampasas a day or two ago, giving me an invitation, or rather making me an offer to once more enter the journalistic field. From what he says, I should judge the opening would be advantageous financially.

I wrote him a confidential letter, telling him candidly that my acceptance depended on two doubtful circumstances. First, whether a certain young lady wanted me, and secondly, whether she would rather live in Lampasas as the wife of a newspaper man, or in Marienfeld as the wife of a wool-grower. If he wished to keep the offer open for a few weeks, these questions could be settled. So you see, you have considerable influence over my movements, whether you appreciate the fact or not.

Goodnight
Yours Affectionately
J.B.M.

* Andrew is Mollie's younger brother. He never married, so it is uncertain who Mary is.

$\partial \!\!\!\!\sim$ 16 $\sim \!\!\!\! \partial$

Marienfeld June 4/89

My Dear Mollie,

I've made it a rule all my life since reaching a letter writing age to be prompt in answering letters. If it were not for this I do not think I should make an effort to write to you tonight, because its rather late, and I'm somewhat tired. Don't think I keep to this rule from a sense of duty, especially with you, for whenever I find myself writing to anyone from a standpoint of this kind, I usually break off the correspondence.

I've been feeling a little "blue" all day. I was informed this morning that "my folks," as I have got to call Mr. Mullinix's family, were going to leave Marienfeld. I've lived with them almost constantly for nine years. Five or six on the ranch when we were in partnership, and since they moved in town I have boarded with them. Have made "pets" out of his children, until the oldest, who is almost a young lady, being too old to pet, I pass a great deal of my time in teasing.

Obeying the promptings of my unfortunate disposition, unfortunate at least for this day and time, I've become very much attached to them. Marienfeld, bad enough before, will be less endurable than ever. I suppose I will have to board at the hotel. If there's any one feature in a lonely man's life more lonely than all else, its occupying a seat regularly at a hotel table.

I went into a young man's room this morning to see him. He's one of the hotel boarders, and I found him busily engaged in repairing an opening in the back of his coat. I've had to do a good-deal of my own cooking the last few years, but in the matter of sewing, I've been lucky. Even the short time I spent in Lampasas, Mrs. Campbell was very kind in this regard. As I told Mr. C., if I could "stand in" as well with the single members of the fair sex as I did with the married, I would have no reason to complain.

I had a letter from [Cousin] Janie this morning, the second, I think, since leaving there. She invites me very cordially to come down to a moon-light picnic, with which she intends to celebrate her birthday.

The picnic, I believe, is on the 11th inst.* Receiving your letter and hers at the same time, each containing an invitation of like character, brings to mind one occasion not very long since, when I *did* treat you very impolitely, to say the least, for the sake of seeing them.

I sometimes wonder if there ever will come a time again, when I *could* unthinkingly leave you to see *any* one else. I guess not.

My going off that Saturday night the last time I was in Austin has given me more cause for regret, I think, than any like act of which I was ever guilty. If the knowledge of the fact that *since* that night, you've not only been first in my thoughts, but almost solely their occupant, will recompense you any for that thoughtlessness, you are certainly nearly "square." That's the last night, I think, that I've gone to sleep comparatively contented and happy.

You've often known me to say that we agreed on a few minor points. It has also been said that "great minds run in the same channel." Your long explanation of why I should proceed to Graham forthwith and not by any means be later than the 21st was, not exactly anticipated, but the same thought had crossed my rather slow intelligence, slow at least when it has to grasp the thought of what people say.

This is the most serious drawback with country towns, that the inhabitants thereof so occupy their minds with the affairs of other people. If they have any concerns of their own, they must be sadly neglected. I'm more considerate, however, where young ladies are concerned, I expect, than most men, and the inhabitants of Graham will spend their time uselessly if they try to make any topics of conversation out of my movements.

I do not think it queer or absurd your writing to me about it. I also appreciate your kindness in saying, come anyway and let the people talk, but I have too much consideration for you to let the "people talk." I cannot say certainly now whether I can come down before the 21st or not, but think it very likely I can. My future movements so as to blind the eyes of your critical friends can be decided later on.

Little Girl, its half past one A.M., and I don't feel nearly so tired as I did when I began this. A little talk to you now and then does a fellow

lots of good in more ways than one. From the way these lines are beginning to lose themselves, tho', and these letters of mine begin to roam,
my eyes, I guess, do not perceive as clearly as they did two hours ago.

Ever Affectionately Yours,
J.B.M.

* The abbreviation *inst.* is an old usage meaning this month.

 17

Marienfeld June 10/89

My Dear Mollie,
   The "affectionate" letter to which I received your reply yesterday,
I somewhat regretted writing at first, but it occasioned such a "nice"
answer from you that I am sorry no more. 'Twas not the affectionate
part, of course, that caused me the regret. I know I have fallen into a
habit of "sorter" *complaining* of your letters and you not being demonstrative enough, and its too much like finding fault to be very agreeable to you. . . .
   I've been doing some very close figuring lately in the matter of time,
trying to solve the long unsolved problem of being in two places at
once, or of doing two days work in one. I have once or twice thought
"I had it," but now have grave reasons to doubt. Two or three days ago
I had everything (I was still calculating at this point) mapped out so I
could leave here next Friday, reach Graham Saturday, stay four days and
get back to Sweetwater, where I have an engagement on the 21st. I had
several things to do here which would take up every day until Friday.
Since making this calculation, I have lost two days, by some unforeseen
things turning up.
   This brings the time of my leaving here down to Sunday, and leaves
me two of the shortest days in the year (considering) to be spent with

you. The chances are very much in favor of even those days being needed for something else, and if they are, I very much fear we will have to explain to the talkative old ladies of Graham why it happened I did not get there sooner.

I'm afraid you'll think my assertion of being able to come any time a rash one, or that I do not want to come. Hardly the latter. However, since writing you that letter, I have made some "trades" that will occupy almost my whole time for the next few weeks.

As I say, there's the possibility that I may come to see you Monday, but just a possibility. I will not speak much of the disappointment because I trust the delay will not be for long, and that you will be all the "gladder" to see me when I do come. As for myself, I guess I want to see you as much now as I possibly could.

June 11 — . . . The weather out here now reminds one of the weather in Austin last winter, in the manner of dampness, and I fear another day will be lost on this account. I guess 'twill be safer considering all things for you not to expect me for some little time. Neither of us, I guess, would get much satisfaction out of the visit, if I were to come in on the stage one evening, and leave next morning. I know you will give me credit for a little candor and honesty, and believe that I have no other reasons for not coming than lack of time.

There were some "drawbacks" occasionally when I would call on you in Austin, but I guess neither of us will ever be the subject of remark outside of relations, and they, of course, will not be unkindly critical.

Yours Affectionately
J.B.M.

NOTE: *In spite of his fears, J.B.M. does get to Graham before June twenty-first. This time he is exceedingly happy about what occurs.*

~ II ~

*My Dear
Little Girl*

18

Thomson House, (Formerly Sikes House.)
J.R. Thomson, Proprietor.
Feather Beds in Winter and South Rooms in Summer.
Good Bath and Sample Rooms.

Weatherford, Texas, June 20, 1889

My Dear Little Girl,
    Notwithstanding the repeated horrors of the stage ride, I am here
with no broken bones, not the least bit tired, and making due allowance
for the distance separating me from you, in the best possible spirits.
    I think for once that retrospection proves almost as pleasant as antic-
ipation. Aside from the fact that *you* have given all earthly things a rose
colored hue, I owe this to your sisters one and all. To say that in making things pleasant in the way of hospitality, *their* kindness is only ex-
ceeded by *yours*, in another direction. The two days in Graham were
very happy ones, and I think they will long be remembered as one of the
pleasant places a man sometimes crosses during his life.
    To show you that I gladly accede to your wishes in regard to your
request of not reporting things to the Austin folks, I will not even write
to *Thad*. It was mostly a matter of pride that I intended it, because,
although you seemed to doubt it, I *do* feel very proud of you. I have
great confidence in Thad's powers of secrecy in most things, but you
know it requires more than average ability in this regard, to keep such
news as I would tell him to himself. So, although it may seem to other
people that I treat it as a matter of no great importance, by keeping
silent, *you* will know better, and *you* are the one I shall consider.
    I am perfectly willing to give you exclusive jurisdiction over the time
and manner of making it known, reserving to myself only the right,
when some of my married lady friends on the plains advise me to get
married, to tell them "I am going to." Possibly I may mention the fact
to some others out there. To this, of course, you will find no objection,
and I very likely shall say nothing about it, because I make confidantes
of very few. If such an unlikely thing should happen that I should *see*

Weatherford, Texas, June 20 1889

My Dear Little Girl,

Notwithstanding the reputed horrors of the stage ride, I am here, with no broken bones, not the least bit tired, and making due allowance for the distance separating me from you, in the best possible spirits. I think for once, that retrospection proves almost as pleasant as anticipation, and aside from the fact that you have given all earthly things a rose colored hue, I owe this to your sisters one and all, to say that in making things pleasant in the way of hospitality, their kindness is only

Thad, I make no rash promise, because you see, Little Girl, its "awful hard" for a fellow to be engulfed in one great sea of happiness and not want some one to rejoice with him.

Thank you ever so much for the improved style of address in your note. It may sound rather soft, but the name never looked so well before.* If I hadn't been anxious to please you anyway, I couldn't have refused your very reasonable request when I could see you were trying to please me.

I only intended this as an answer to your note, but My Dear, *Dear* Little Sweetheart, its hard to tell you good-bye even on paper.

Affectionately Yours,

J.B.M.

---

* Perhaps she used "John" for the first time. To other people she will refer to him always as "Mr. McGill."

 19

[Postmarked Colorado, Texas]
"Under the wagon"
June 24, 1889

My Dear Little Girl,

I commenced a letter to you last night, but after baking my head before the fire for a few minutes, and knowing I should have ample time during the day to write, I adjourned and went to bed. I flatter myself you will be waiting for this. It's an awful nice thought for a fellow to indulge in, that a little girl somewhere in the world likes to hear from him. I don't feel half as lonesome now when I only have my own thoughts for a companion, as I did before I could comfort myself with the fact that I was frequently the subject of your meditations, as you are nearly always the subject of mine.

My anxiety now has taken a different turn. I have been so elevated above this vale of tears, and rendered so supremely happy by my last talks with you, that it doesn't seem possible hardly for it to last. I feel as much above my average state of being, in the way of felicity, as I once felt below it in the way of misery when I was respectfully declined with*out* thanks, by you. I think you realized that I was considerably cast down, then.

I frequently have the feeling that you no doubt have often had. When you would hear of something to take place of which you had very pleasant anticipations, you would "kinder" *fear* something might occur to prevent it. What the result to me would be in this case if that *something should* occur, I cannot form the slightest idea. I can realize now the force of a remark Thad made to me last winter. We were discussing our different situations, when he says, "Yes, you think it hard to have to give up a girl you have only thought of for a few *weeks*. What do you suppose I should do if I had to give up one I've been *engaged* to for four *years*."

I don't mean you to infer that it seems four years since last week, altho' time does pass slowly sometimes, but I guess 'twould be a little harder to think of giving you up now than before, and 'twas *hard* before. With all due respect to Thad's powers of affection, I don't think his wife of a few months after an engagement of four years, is any more loved than is My Little Girl at the present moment.

I expect if a third person were to peruse my letters to you they would think I made rather unlimited use of the first and second personal pronouns, but I gather from a remark you made, that my missives had had some influence with you in the right direction. So if the third person's criticism be just or unjust, I will still continue to write about ourselves. I guess for this issue, however, even *you* will think it hard for me to get on to any other subject. Well, you'd think correctly, but I will make an effort.

Everything so far on the trip is progressing smoothly. This time I have two men with somewhat different nationalities than my Mexican. One is a German who brought the wagon down from Marienfeld, and the other I suppose claims the United States as his native land. I haven't much to do myself except to give orders and think (about you principally).

I have other thoughts occasionally, however, and one today about myself I expect will appear somewhat conceited. It is, that I'm kinder to animals under my control, and take greater delight in seeing them, "animally" speaking, happy, than almost any man whom I've known in like situations. This thought came to me today (not for the first time I expect) while watching the sheep drink from a lake of water by the roadside.

They had been nearly two days without water, and while not suffering, were very thirsty. They waded into the water, some almost swimming, and seemed to enjoy it so, that I felt almost as much satisfaction as if I were having my own thirst quenched.

Another thought came to me at the same time, how much in some respects a flock of sheep were like the same number of people. The lake was quite muddy on its banks, and while quite a lot of them walked right into it, and drank without any hesitation, a great many "meandered" up and down the water's edge looking for a place to get to it without wetting their feet. Others would take a sip at one place and its not tasting exactly right, they would go to another spot. All, you understand, very thirsty, but would be fastidious at the expense of their comfort.

Another conceited idea has impressed itself on my mind since yesterday, and that is my honesty compared with others who have like temptations. I know you will say that honesty is honesty and there is no half way ground. Neither does there ever arise any condition when a man would be justifiable in being dishonest, also that I have no cause for conceit. I agree with you all the way thro', but you must remember *your* views are those of one of the most honest little girls I ever knew (as I told you before), and the views of men who buy and sell, especially live stock, are as different from yours as right from wrong.

The temptation under which I'm struggling is simply this. The men from whom I bought the sheep are excessively close. I dislike to trade with such men, because I seldom trust *their* honesty and am compelled to watch them constantly. While separating and counting the flock I could see very readily they were trying to take advantage of me whenever they could, and I gave up to them in several instances rather than count a certain lot of sheep twice, or argue the matter. After the number was settled we figured up the amount due.

They did their calculating on paper, and while I usually do mine in my head, this time for some reason I did not. But when their calculation was handed me, I looked it over, very carelessly I guess, and pronounced it right. After I had settled up and come away, I began a little mental calculation, and soon discovered an error of twenty dollars in my favor.

The chances are they will never go over their figures again. So you see, altho' its no temptation to steal $20.00, it is somewhat of a temptation to "get even" with men who you *know* have tried to steal from you.

I think my ambition in regard to the length of this letter should now be satisfied. I began on a green page and have been energetically writing ever since on different colors with the fond hopes that my stock of words would last as long as the stock of colors in this tablet, so that I might have two leaves the same shade in my letter. If the substance of this epistle proves of a sameness, I trust the paper on which it is written will break the monotony.

I cannot tell you yet when I can get a letter from you. As I am traveling faster than I expected, unless something prevents, I will reach M- much sooner than July 8th- which I think was the date I told you. I will let you know, however, in time so I will not have to wait any longer than necessary. I will try to get this on the train tomorrow. If I do not I will have to mail it in Colorado [City] next day, being about twelve miles east of that city at present writing.

If I don't end this now I will be drifting back again to "U" and I. I feel the pressure to tell you some more that "I love U," so great, that I cannot resist much longer, so good-bye.

Yours Affectionately,
J.B.M.

I delayed this one day rather than use this envelope, but the P.O. in Colorado [City] is closed and I guess you will excuse appearances considering.   J—

Rotan, June 28/89

My Dear Little Girl,

I feel somewhat provoked at myself for not writing you yesterday during the hours when the sun shines brightest, instead of passing most of the time sleeping, but I thought 'twould be noon today when I reached this station. And instead, I drove up not much after seven o' clock, just in time to see the east-bound passenger train leave, which would have taken this letter had it been written. The result is very serious. In the first place I must write *you* a very short letter, because I can't stop here long, and no other depot between here and Big Springs. In the second, owing to the fact that no stage runs on Sunday, you cannot receive this before Monday night, and I will have to wait two days after I reach M— before I can hear from you. I expect to get there Tuesday, but a man engaged in this occupation cannot time himself as accurately as he can in some others.

The rate of speed depends on so many circumstances that it is very likely to vary. The weather since leaving Sweetwater has been so favorable, being cool and cloudy, that so far, more progress has been made than I thought likely. There being no moon-light, my nights have passed more satisfactorily than was the case when I came up six week ago. A rain storm Monday night caused some loss of sleep, but I am making it up during the day. All these favorable circumstances, however, do not prevent this excursion proving monotonous, and I shall rejoice (moderately) when 'tis over.

I have frequently thought that if some of the non-admirers of the Graham stage could start out on a trip of this kind, where I've been over five days traveling forty-eight miles, they would think the stage a lightning express, comparatively.

I don't want you to think that I'm falling off in my regard, because I send you such a poor excuse for a letter as this, but I'm stopped in the road with the horses hitched to the wagon and if I wait until noon 'twill be too far to come back to mail it.

I know you will make due allowance for everything. I promise when the next forty miles are over with, and I once more take a letter from the post office addressed in your familiar hand-writing, which has grown inexpressively dear to me, I will endeavor to improve.

Remember me with kindest regards to my cousins. For the present, my Little Sweetheart, good-bye.

Very Faithfully Yours,
J.B.M.

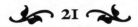 21

Marienfeld, July 4, 1889

My Dear Mollie,

I am certainly having things all my own way in the letter writing line, but it's growing a little wearing. I wish I had not been so considerate in my instructions to you about when to write, but I dislike to wait for an answer to a letter myself, and did not want to make you wait. I thought when I wrote last I would not inflict any more of my epistles upon you, until I rec'd yours, but it's not the first time, as you well know, that my resolutions in this direction have been broken. I was thinking of writing last night, but was, to use a western phrase "completely played out."

I had about a ten miles walk after a run-away team, and then had to borrow a horse from the nearest ranch to ride after it. My buggy ponies had been used very little during my absence, and yesterday evening I harnessed them to the wagon and very carelessly left them standing with no one holding the "lines." The result was as before stated.

When I came in town this morning I was informed that the Rail-Road was out of repair in the neighborhood of Weatherford, owing to heavy rains, and that our mail from the east would be scarce for a while. Then I *knew* I would have to talk to you before your letter came, even if it was little one-sided.

Marienfeld is celebrating the Fourth-but The Deserted Village would be a London, comparatively, even when we are celebrating.* The state of affairs here, numerically speaking, in the way of inhabitants is simply appalling. I reached town yesterday morning, or rather the evening of the day before. I camped about two miles east of town, Tuesday night, and came in horse-back for supper. Camp-diet was growing very monotonous, and altho' this hotel is not noted for its fare, I thought supper that night an excellent meal. Today for dinner, however, it surpassed itself, and I thoroughly enjoyed the celebration that far.

Judge Allan, and the school teacher, I think, are the only *young* men, Americans, left here now. Mr. Cutler, whose paper I'm utilizing, and two or three more are summering in other regions, and if I didn't have so much on my hands, very likely I should be summering somewhere else.

When I think the next few months will end this way of living, and that instead of a boarding house or a hotel, I will have a *home*, and the dearest little girl I ever knew for a companion, 'tis not wonderful I should be happy. It's over twenty years since I had a *home*. From the time a boy loses his mother until as a man he gets a wife, altho' he may find plenty of pleasant resting places, a *home* in the true sense of the word he has none.

At this point I was interrupted and had to talk "business" with a man for some time. My ideas have been so scattered that I expect if I write much longer such a change will be observable that you'll think its not the same fellow writing.

I believe I can promise you this time certainly that I will wait until you write before I bother you again. But if I should fail to keep it, I'm happy in the thought that you appreciate my inability to keep silence long.

Yours Affectionately,
J.B.M.

* "The Deserted Village" is a poem by Oliver Goldsmith. J.B.M. obviously enjoys using literary allusions.

Marienfeld July 7 '89

My Dear Mollie,

Owing to delayed mails, and to my not being able to visit the P.O. for a day or two, your letter of the 2nd was not rec'd until today. To say 'twas most welcome would be expressing myself in a very limited manner.

I'm inclined to believe that your reason for not having a letter or two waiting for me when I arrived here, is one that has frequently influenced you in our intercourse with each other. I would like now to relieve your mind of any such fear, for all time to come, and say that unless a very great change takes place in both of us, you will never appear silly to me. I think I wrote to you four times after I left Graham before I rec'd your letter today. And if you had written as often to me, and I had taken all from the office at once, I would simply have thought, "Well, my Little Girl thinks more of me than I believed she did." So whenever the "spirit moves" you in future to write to me, rest assured that *I* will never think you write too often.

I've been rather busy since I came back. Found lots of work which I left to be done while I was away, not half done, consequently I'm somewhat crowded. Water is the great trouble, and as the people of this section are not noted for speed, it takes more time to get anything done, than it would elsewhere. I'm somewhat under the impression that I have just about as much on my hands as I can well attend to; but guess I'll pull thro' all right.

I went to Midland yesterday, and renewed my acquaintance with some of its inhabitants. Had several invitations to come out there and abide, and informed all "inviters" that such was my intention. I had to call on one of my lady acquaintances for the use of her needle and thread. I expect the circumstance will prove amusing to you.

On the road out, I got out of the buggy for something, and as I placed my foot on the step to get in again, the horses started (in a run, of course). I made a jump and not having on any coat, caught the armhole of my vest on the buggy top. I had no time to unfasten it, and the result was, when I took my seat in the vehicle again, the garment was torn from top to bottom.

I drove up to the feed-stable and after unhitching the horses, I asked the proprietor if he could loan me a paper of pins. He said "just go in the house, and ask Mrs. Collins," his wife, "to sew it up." I was not very well acquainted with her, and don't think I'd ever been in the house before, but concluded I'd take him at his word, so walked to the kitchen door where she was busy, and made my request. She took it as an every-day occurrence, and told me to go in the parlor and have a seat while she did the repairing. I followed her instructions, and she soon brought me in the vest, as good as new. I expected all the time to hear her say I ought to have a wife, but I guess she thought 'twould sound as if *she* didn't like the job.

I ate dinner with Mrs. Mullinix and family, and found them very comfortably settled, and very well satisfied with the change from Marienfeld. Mr. M— has gone into the grocery business, but says he finds it harder work than running a sheep-ranch. I didn't stay in town long, and came back in the afternoon.

We are having a remarkable summer for this region, but I guess I'll not go into particulars on the *weather*. I'll reserve that subject for some future occasion, if I should happen to need it, for some correspondent to whom I haven't anything to say.

I agree with you, that if Mary says "Cousin Andrew," the fond anticipations in which both parties seemed for a season to indulge, are very likely fond anticipations no more. For to my certain knowledge she called him "Andrew," pure and simple, when she first met him; therefore, their last state must be worse than the first.

It's something entirely beyond my comprehension, how most people love. I guess I'm differently constituted from the majority, but with the utmost stretch of the imagination I couldn't picture to myself life worth living if I thought a time would come when you and I could be simply cousins to each other again. To put it in plain English, and without any conceit, I think there are very few men who *can* love as I do. I don't believe *you* ever have, and very likely you never will, fully realize how completely my life is centered in you.

Mary wouldn't impress one with the idea that she was a girl who would love lightly, but appearances are deceptive sometimes. She was engaged to *one* fellow a few years ago that I know of, possibly there may have been several more.

I'm sorry my colored paper was damaged on the road by dampness, you seem to appreciate it. But I trust that through all our lives our material surroundings will have as little effect on our appreciation of each other, as does now the color of the paper have on the appreciation of each other's letters.

Goodnight,

Yours Affectionately,
J.B.M.

 23

Marienfeld July 12/89

My Dear Mollie,

For the same reasons given in my last, your letter did not reach me until today. I was disappointed Wednesday, because I supposed you'd write Sunday, and it should have been here Tuesday night, but I guess 'twas "side-tracked" on the road. I could not get to the Post Office yesterday, but was rewarded this morning.

Your letters are much more satisfactory than they "used to be," and while I always looked forward to them with the greatest impatience, still as I expect you were frequently made to feel, they left me after perusing them in rather a fault-finding mood. I can't exactly explain the difference now. *Possibly* the difference may lie in some other direction, but I realize this fact; there is no desire in my mind now-a-days to give you any instructions as to how you ought to write. If I "fussed" at *you* any, because I had to wait a few days for your first letter, the item has escaped my memory.

I'm always exceedingly careful about what I say, ever since you translated what I said about a "weak intellect," into a reflection on yourself. You know you never have been quite as out-spoken as your sister, Cousin Lulu, was in regard to Dr. James, so I don't know how much of a "hold" I've got on *you*. Our ideas of engagements, I remember, differed considerably, so at any time you might destroy all my hopes, by informing me that the other fellow for whom you had greater love had turned up. Consequently I shall not dare to fuss, criticize, find fault, be sarcastic, complain, or make fun, until I have you securely. *Then* Little Girl, I expect I'll love you so well, that I'll not have any will of my own, but be very submissive.

If I'd had any great admiration for the Mrs. Copperfield style of women, then this epistle, and many others, would never have been written.* I always thought the only act Dora performed which deserved any commendation was to take her departure from this "vale of tears," and give David a chance to marry a woman, who, with one or two exceptions, was the only *good* woman character Dickens ever put into his books. The only two women of my acquaintance of whom I can think right now that in any way are of the Dora "style of beauty," are Mrs. B.T. Bell and her younger sister. I don't know her husband's name. I believe I've expressed to you, most too freely I guess, my admiration (!) for them.

In the early days of our acquaintance, I told you, I think, one of the first things I desired in a wife, was to get a woman I could "talk to," and if I couldn't get one of this kind, I should live it out "sad and alone." I guess you'll discover on our pilgrimage that you will occupy the place of *partner* in every sense of the word to a greater extent than wives generally do. I don't mean that women should do men's work, figuratively or literally, but I'm one of the few men who believe that a woman's ideas are frequently better than his own. Are "them" your sentiments, Little Girl?

Water-melons are beginning to put in an appearance in this section. These are about the only variety of fruit this country produces, so far, but great hopes are held by many that it will finally be second only to California in its vineyards and orchards. I've never been a strong believer in this, but experiments in this direction are turning out very encouragingly. If such should be the case, then I guess neither of us will regret making it our stopping place. I trust tho' we will have no cause for regret even if this desirable change does not take place.

I wrote to Mr. Campbell a few days ago, and told him that your preference being one with mine, his offer could not be accepted. I don't know what he'll have to say.

The more I ponder over the present situation of ourselves, the more I wonder how Thad managed to exist four long years, especially while he was absent under similar circumstances. I can see how a fellow could manage to pull along moderately easy when he was near his girl, and could call on her two or three times a day. Even then 'twould likely try his patience. But to be absent for thirteen months at one time, seems to me would be too much for this individual. Its been three weeks since I left Graham, and I'm growing terribly homesick already. I *know* I couldn't stand it twelve months and one week longer.

I think my judgment in regard to your picture, not wanting one when I left Austin, but very anxious for it the last time, very sensible. If I'd had it all through the trying time before I went to Graham, 'twould have worried me much more, to have been reminded each time I looked at it of what I had lost. But now everything is different.

When I reached Sweetwater on my way back, I sent my valise up by express, with the picture inside. One of the first things I did on reaching M— was to get the valise from the office and take a long look at the photo. I don't know whether you call this silly or not, but I can't help it, Little Girl.

Yours Affectionately,
J.B.M.

* In Charles Dickens' novel, *David Copperfield*, Dora Copperfield is a pretty, empty-headed girl. After her death, David marries Agnes Wickfield, sweet, loving and intelligent.

≫ 24 ≪

Marienfeld July 15th 1889.

My Dear Mollie,

Its very satisfactory to have a correspondent that you can rely upon, so that when you call for a letter you'll not be disappointed, or if you are, you can rest perfectly easy that the fault is in the mail. I never enjoyed this blessing before, and find it now something to truly appreciate. Letters lose a great deal of their attraction when you wait for them from week to week. . . .

Your letter received today had an item in it quite flattering and at the same time a trifle humiliating, but the gratification so far over-balances the humiliation, that you need not worry. 'Twas in saying you did not know whether I intended to make you live on a ranch or in town. I think when a woman thinks enough of a man to be *willing* to live on a ranch for his sake, he should be perfectly satisfied with her regard and not ask any other sacrifice to prove it. Herein lies the flattery.

You don't know as I do, of course, the hardships (I don't mean particularly physical) that a woman undergoes spending her existence, or a few years of it, on a ranch in western Texas. The humiliation lies in the fact that you supposed I would be cruel enough to let you undergo any such trials and tribulations, if I could help it. Of course, all things in this life are uncertain, and the wool-growing business is no exception. The time might come when you and I would be keeping house in a little 10 x 12 shanty on the prairie. I don't imagine any such time ever will come, but when it does, I'll venture to make the assertion that your spirits, like mine have heretofore done, will rise to the occasion, and that the handsomest residences in the large cities will not hold two happier people than will our little cabin.

I'm not as positive, however, about Midland being our future home as I was. I expect you'll begin to think that I'm given to frequent changes of mind, but it's not this at all. Isn't there something about necessity knowing no law? I have been under the impression all the time that I could locate somewhere near enough to Midland to make that place home, and thought I knew the place where I would have a well dug. But after I had contracted to have a boring machine go to work, I yesterday evening took a ride over the ground (hadn't seen it for two or three years), and concluded 'twouldn't do.

Tomorrow or next day, I shall start out on a tour of observation, and see where the largest unappropriated country is. If possible, I would like to have the ranch near enough to where we live so that I could drive to it and return in one day, but whether I shall succeed or not remains to be "saw."

I'm going out in the neighborhood of the first city west of Midland, a town I've never yet visited, called on rail-road maps "Odessa," and called in advertising circulars "Nature's Sanitarium" or "The Health Resort of the Plains."

There are two things necessary, one is to find a place not *too unpleasant* for our home and the other, a place not too unpleasant for our supporters, the sheep. Heretofore the latter consideration has been my only care, and if I succeed as well in the former duty, or rather pleasure, as in this we will not complain. I remember you informed me that your surroundings had very little to do with your happiness, but notwithstanding this assertion, I prefer they should be as pleasant as we can make them. I wish all arrangements were over with and we were settled down. In fact, I wish we had been settled down three or four years ago. I feel as if several years of happiness might have been gained if this could have been.

I believe they had church at Marienfeld yesterday, but I did not know of it until I went in town, and did not have on my Sunday clothes. The same man I think, preached, of whom I wrote you before, so I did not miss much.

I stopped in at Mrs. Karr's, the lady I told you was out at the Midland dance, and she said she supposed he was a *good* man, a remark very similar to some Aunt Kate makes. She also made a remark which I did not think called for, if she intended it as it sounded to me. I said something about so many people leaving Marienfeld. "Yes," she says "but just as many are coming in. There is one of the nicest families I ever saw here now and I wouldn't care if some more would leave and let somebody come who had a little intelligence and taste."

TEXAS.

THE NEW SOUTHWEST, THE NEW COUNTY OF ECTOR

—THE—

NEW TOWN OF ODESSA.

Fine Opportunities to Secure Cheap Homes. Many
Advantages to Men of Family. Provisions have
been made for Colleges, Library, Public
Schools, Churches, &c.

NO SALOONS.

The Staked Plain of West Texas

Are found Rich Land, Pure Water, and the Best All-
the-Year Climate in the World.

———

ODESSA LAND AND TOWN-SITE CO
JANUARY 1, 1888

*This booklet was distributed by a group of developers from Ohio who called them-
selves the "Odessa Land and Town-site Company." Dated January 1, 1888, it
contains a great deal of fulsome praise for the area, most of the "facts" unrelated to
the actual situation. Courtesy Ector County Library, Odessa, Texas.*

Now the *nice* family occupy the house Mr. Mullinix lived in and I know Mrs. Karr and Mrs. Mullinix were on very friendly terms. I must ask Mrs. M— the next time I see her what the falling out was about. Its quite amusing sometimes to stand on one side and watch these little battles.

My regards to your sisters.

Yours Affectionately,
J.B.M.

I will likely be absent four or five days, so if your next letter is not answered immediately, 'twill be for this reason. I will not place any restrictions on you 'tho in regard to answering this.

Good-bye.
J.

Marienfeld, July 19, 1889

My Dear Little Girl,

You will no doubt be surprised to a moderate extent, after my telling you in my last letter not to expect an answer to yours rec'd today at once, to get this, but my trip west has been postponed until, I expect, tomorrow. Rather I should say I intend to start tomorrow. It's now getting towards the last hours of today. I *did* make an effort to go the day I intended, but when I was three or four miles on the road, a man overtook me, and imparted the information that he wished to buy some sheep. The opportunity to make an honest dollar was not to be thrown away, so I returned, and am here yet, and will give you the benefit of part of the time.

If the repetition of an assertion several times does not grow monotonous, let me say once more that your letters are becoming more and more satisfactory. I frequently wonder now-a-days how I ever called you a little ice-berg, but you *are* changing, there is no doubt about this. I've been waiting patiently for you to sign yourself "affectionately" and you last letter is so closed.

I know with ninety-nine people out of a hundred, this does not signify anything. Their letters are signed in this style either from force of habit, or because they wish to *appear* affectionate. I know you are the one hundredth, and when you closed your last letter saying "affectionately" I know you were thinking a "good-deal" of me.

It's a very pleasant thought for me to indulge in, My Little Girl, that you are beginning to love me a little. It's like a person who has been starving for some time, always in sight of some tempting viand, finally having a delicate morsel given him, with the hopes held out that very soon he can take a seat at a well filled table. I loved *you* for what seemed to me a long, long time, with very small hopes held out that you would ever return it, never for a moment believing the theory which you had of yourself that you *couldn't* love, but doubting very seriously at times if 'twas in me to awaken any regard in you. I don't appreciate you any less, you may be sure of this fact, because you were hard to get.

If your cousin Frank loves you as I do, then indeed I feel sorry for him. But he can't, that's all, or he couldn't take "no" quite so easily. I think you place too literal a construction on many things I've said to you.

I don't remember now what called forth the remark that I could see no difference in a man's making love to my sweetheart, and in making love to my wife, but certainly I couldn't mean this literally. You can't help a fellow's loving you, neither can that fellow help himself. I know this from experience. I guess I meant that a girl should give a man no encouragement when she was engaged to another.

Don't take this to yourself please, Little Girl, and don't apply anything else that I *have* said or that I *may* say to yourself. I don't think I shall ever have any instructions to give you. If you could only know how well I like you just as you are, then none of my general remarks would make you have any desire to change for my benefit.

I have written a letter to your father which I send in this to you. I do not know his address, and if you do not care to address it to him yourself, you can return it and I will mail it from here. My reasons for not writing to him before are just what I told him. I leave the document open and if you feel inclined to know what I think of you before a third party you are perfectly welcome to learn. I am not satisfied with the letter, but I guess a short and plain statement of facts is all that's necessary.*

If I had not agreed with you that we should not apologize for our letters to each other, I would say I'm not satisfied with *this*, but I can't write tonight, and I know you'd rather have this than wait.

Affectionately Yours,

J.B.M.

July 20. My intention today, when I discovered that I had a few minutes at my disposal, was to destroy this missive and reconstruct another, but when I considered nearly all last night was spent in its composition I concluded to let it go.

I suppose the trouble with me last night was that letter to your father. I wrote one to him first, then began yours, thinking the whole time of the one first written. When this was half through I quit, and wrote another to him which did not suit me as well as the first. Finally, I guess about two-o'clock in the morning, I closed this one as you observe much disgusted with myself, and went to bed.

I have just finished my third one to Judge McCormick which, altho' I have serious doubts about, I guess will have to go also. I am altogether ignorant of the correct manner of doing these things, but I shouldn't think 'twould appear strange for you to address my letter to him telling him why I did not send it direct.

It's growing towards evening, and I must drive to Midland tonight so for a second time I will say good-bye.

Unless something else stops me, I expect my explanation in my last letter will be good for this.

Yours,

J.

---

* Unfortunately, this guess is far from accurate.

🔈 26 🔊

Marienfeld, July 25, 1889

My Dear Little Girl,
    . . . I came into the ranch late last night after meandering over the country for several days. If I had started to Graham Saturday noon and had traveled as far in that direction since then as I have in others, I think very likely I would have been near enough to do away with letter writing.
    If I look at this country a few years longer I guess not much of it will be unknown. Odessa was duly inspected, as was the surrounding country. Both were pronounced undesirable. I think, tho', the *healthy* reputation very likely deserved. One lonely looking grave in the prairie was all I could see in the way of a cemetery.
    I came back to Midland with the determination to settle the question of our abode by investing in enough ground to hold a house, but did not have time to attend to it. I shall, however, I think, the next time I go there. Midland is different from most western towns from the fact that it is made up of a better class of people than new towns usually are. I heard one man say the other day, who is rather given to profanity, that he was getting ashamed of himself, that he could stand on the streets all day and seldom hear an oath. I told him 'twas a good thing that the Texas and Pacific [Railroad] could boast of having one respectable town.
    One very great advantage, so far as I am concerned and I guess we are the same, is that in Midland we can get something to eat. Marienfeld is the poorest place I ever saw in this regard. Not being enough people here to keep fresh meat, nor express fresh vegetables, makes the town no better than the country. I appreciate good living to quite an extent, but I guess I live about as hard as a man well can, who *could* afford better. During this last trip, one or two square meals in Midland, and I fared tolerably well at the Odessa Hotel, were all I could boast of in the way of eating. I ate several times at ranches, and generally at these places a fellow eats merely because he has to.
    One expression in your letter reminds me very forcibly of what I

have done nearly all my life, and is one that I use frequently, "take my chances." If I were as certain in all the chances that I *do* take, that the end would be as I desired, as I feel in taking you, that no cause for regret would ever arise, then my ventures would be entered into with a feeling of security seldom felt. *You* take more chances than I do, and *this* in fact is the only risk I assume, whether or not you will ever wish things could be changed.

Personally I run no risk whatever. My life before I knew you was worthless to anyone else, and while I had no desire to end it, it was not particularly attractive to me. *Now* if I had to go back to the old state of things, with the memory of you fresh in my mind, then my existence would be more valuable to some entire stranger than to myself.

No, My Little Sweetheart, your fears should be centered on yourself, not on me. I feel as perfectly secure in my hopes for the future, so far as you being the woman I need are concerned, that I rest very easy.

Very Affectionately,
J.B.M.

 27

Marienfeld, July 27, 1889

My Dear Mollie,

I've visited the Post Office now, twice, with the expectation of a letter from you and twice have I been disappointed. I fear my praise in regard to your promptness had a bad effect, or possibly another lame finger is the cause. Anything reasonable in the way of excuse for this silence and I will grant you free pardon, but nothing such as want of time, no news, etc. will pass with me now. Your letters form too great a part of my happiness for me to be disappointed in this way without complaint. . . .

I had a letter from Mr. Dumble this morning, the first time I've heard from him, and the answering of his letter, in the way I will have to reply, is rather unpleasant. Fortunately, an unpleasant reply is more easily written than given verbally. I loaned him money last fall and he writes me that he is totally unable to pay the note when it's due and wants an extension of time. Luckily for me, his father in Houston is more reliable, and his name is also signed to the document. A letter from Mr. Campbell a few days ago gave me the information that Dumble was, to use a common expression, "going to the dogs," was doing nothing, and trying to do nothing. So I guess, as I am not a money lender *yet*, I will tell Mr. D. his father's money will be as acceptable as his own. I feel sorry for his wife, even if she *does* happen to be a woman for whom I never formed any great admiration.

I find myself frequently at a loss to know how much of my business affairs to put in my letters to you and how much not to put in . . . .

In this business, more than any other of which I know, men will talk over their affairs with greater freedom, and boast to each other of how well their flocks look. Every one far and near will know as much of his neighbor's affairs as his neighbor knows of them himself. In this section of country there is no other subject discussed among the majority than sheep and wool, and I've so often seen men who *couldn't* talk of anything else that I keep clear of the theme as much as possible. It's likely to grow monotonous after a while. The questions, "How are your sheep?" and "How are your cattle?" are asked about as often here as "How are crops?" is asked in the East.

It's curious to notice, tho', how much of a hold the business of the people of any locality will get on the minds of its inhabitants. I see this everywhere I go. In traveling over Texas every hundred miles or so, as you sit around a hotel or other public place, you can easily know what the chief industry is in that place, and can see it's different from the one just left.

In a new country like this, it's also curious to note the changes of industries as time progresses. In Abilene when I first knew it, 'twas the same as Midland is now, nothing thought of to any extent but stock. Now it's wheat and oats, and the stock-man, like his predecessor the Indian, has moved west. I've no doubt in a few years a wool-grower or cattle-man will feel lonesome on the plains, more so than he does now, from a different cause, however. . . .

If my theory in regard to our letters is right, about the less affectionate I am, the nicer you are, then your answer to this should be highly satisfactory. I haven't loved you any at all in this, have I, Little Girl? But I *do* love you all the same, and not many more moons will grow old, before I come down and tell you this in person.

Now laying all jokes aside about your silence, I *am* disappointed when you don't write, and can't help feeling uneasy.

Yours Affectionately,

J.B.M.

Marienfeld, July 30, 1889

My Dear Mollie,

I suppose you'll think I'm retaliating by this letter being a few days late, but I rec'd yours only this morning. I was certain I should have a letter from you Sunday. Not having a horse convenient I walked about three miles to the office, and found an empty box. The sun was terribly warm, too. I didn't feel it so much going in, and if I'd not had the walk in vain, very likely the heat would not have been noticed at all. I see by the date of yours that it *should* have been here Sunday, so you are not to blame. Yesterday I didn't go to town, so waited a day longer than was necessary before hearing from you.

After returning Sunday afternoon, not having a fresh letter from you, I took the package containing all your old ones and read them through from first to last in regular order, beginning at the first rec'd in Lampasas and ending with that read last week. I guess I'd read each one before at least three times, but I found them very interesting, and derived quite a lot of satisfaction out of them in noting the change from first to last, as also the increased number during the last few weeks. Only one with the date of February, increasing to six in July, counting the one rec'd today.

Their contents brought to mind many things I had written myself to you, and I guess the last few months have wrought quite a change in both of us, more in you than me, however. It must have been in my second letter, I think, judging from yours, where I said I could not write any sentimental nonsense and indulge in extravagant expressions of undying regard. In your reply you say you suppose its very pleasant for people so constituted to enjoy it, to entertain each other in this style, but you think or *thought* it the perfection of silliness.

I expect to a third party, some of my letters since then would seem to lean towards extravagance and sentiment, and to them might appear silly. But to me they certainly do not contain any nonsense, but a truthful statement of facts, and to you I think they do not seem silly.

I guess, Little Girl, we are not so very different from others in the matter of affection, after all. I've come to the conclusion, since loving you, that it's not possible for a man to love a woman and not let her know it constantly, by some means. Whatever these means be, they will likely appear silly to lookers on, but to the two who stand alone, as regards this matter, from the rest of the whole world, their demonstrations of affection for each other come nearer making this earth a heaven of happiness than any other actions of their lives.

I was very much amused at your criticism of my letter to Judge McCormick, and I expect it's rather as you say, but altho' my acquaintance with him is rather limited, I should say he will not have any less respect for a fellow because he is independent.[1] You are the only person I've ever known before whom my independence fades away and I become an asker of favors. Altho' I've always thought that I never would see the woman who could cause me to lose this characteristic, I know better now.

You've heard me applaud Thad in regard to his course about Miss Florence's dancing, and also know how I dislike round dancing.[2] But if you attended balls twice every week and favored every fellow present with a dance, while 'twould hurt me considerably, it would be an utter impossibility for me to tell you, you must either give up the balls or give me up, if I had any idea you would do the latter.

I can never control your actions, even if such an unlikely thing should happen that I should want to, by taking a course similar to the above. I realize this fact thoroughly but it doesn't trouble me in the slightest, because I cannot conceive with the greatest stretch of the imagination that you will ever do anything that will not have my entire endorsement.

I should have answered any letter your father wrote me promptly anyway. I always do this so far as possible, but I'm glad you mentioned it. Little Sweetheart, when you make any suggestion to me or ask me to do anything, please don't feel called upon to make any explanation. I like it, and will never think you are trying to manage my affairs, any more than I want you to. I want you to feel always at perfect liberty to say exactly what you think, and treat me now as you will treat me after a while, as a friend above all earthly friends who will regard all you say to him and all your actions toward him as inspired by feelings of confidence and affection.

Now let me express my sentiments about what I would like *you* to do. Postpone any anticipated ride behind wild horses until *I* drive them and you will never cause me or any one else any uneasiness. When I use a horse that is not perfectly reliable, I will drive it alone, or with another man. This letter is too long to begin a discourse on horses, but I will say that wild animals of this class are dangerous always, and under all circumstances, when they are being handled.[3]

I feel in a writing mood this evening, but guess this is lengthened out enough.

Yours Affectionately,
J.B.M.

[1] This, also, will prove an incorrect assumption.

[2] Apparently Thad gave his fiancee an ultimatum about round or "ballroom" dancing (as opposed to square dancing).

[3] Mollie obviously had been frightened by a run-away buggy ride, when either she or another girl was driving. Fatal accidents were all too common and it is not surprising JBM is concerned.

꧁ 29 ꧂

Marienfeld, August 1st, 1889

My Dear Mollie,

Your reasons for my not getting your letter yesterday are very good, especially the headache. I don't want you to try to write me when you have one, altho' I do happen to be disappointed. I wish such a thing were possible that when you give yourself to me you could also transfer some of those headaches from which you so often suffer.[1] I never had anything like a severe one in my life, and while I do not "hanker" after physical pain, or any other kind, I think I should actually enjoy a headache if I knew 'twas giving you a resting spell.

We will hope that a change of climate will have a healing effect and that you will suffer less when your place of residence is at a higher elevation. With all its drawbacks, a person's health is so good out here and one feels so well, that I believe I'd take it as a dwelling place in preference to any other part of the state.

I guess I'll take you at your word tonight and, in answering your question in regard to a ranch, discourse at some length on affairs generally. I know it's not very satisfactory to have a person write of anything of which you are to a certain extent ignorant. While I'll wait until later before going into details, I will try to make my surroundings more familiar.

When I left here last fall I sold everything, ranch and horses included, reserving only about 1100 sheep which were being taken care of by another man. So when I returned here last winter, I had no stopping place whatever of my own. I became tired of Marienfeld and, needing some help to break those two horses, which are not broken yet, I moved out to this man's ranch intending to go back to town again in a few weeks. This was about the first of April and the few weeks haven't expired yet. So far as Marienfeld is concerned, [they] never will expire.

This ranch is about 3 miles from town and has been my head-quarters all the summer. When I bought the sheep that I now have, I brought them out here in this neighborhood, dug a well, and put up a windmill for temporary use, hardly knowing what would be done in future.

After I had seen you, I then realized that everything, both for ourselves and sheep, must be reconstructed and put on a more solid foundation, and have been taking observations with this end in view. Heretofore I've been like all my neighbors, controlling no land whatever, but "taking my chances" by depending on "free grass."[2] Now very few people in the eastern towns have any idea about the extent of territory required for a "sheep ranch" even of moderate size. Tho' your ideas are the same as mine in many respects, I know you haven't been calculating on the number of acres for a sheep *very* long so possibly you may be somewhat in the dark.

I was talking to the hotel landlady in Odessa the other day, and told her, of course, the object of my visit, that is, I was looking for a location for a sheep ranch. She says, "I don't think you'll have any trouble. Most anyone around here can tell you where you can find a good section of land." I said I thought it very likely, but I needed more than one section.

A section is 640 acres, and in dry times might support 100 sheep. As I want territory for at least 4000 you see *her* ideas of a sheep ranch were hardly advanced enough.

I didn't intend to convey the impression that my search last week was altogether in vain, but only so far as the Odessa country was concerned. I took a ride up north of Midland some 30 miles or so and was quite well satisfied with the country; but do not know yet whether I can get the land or not. Mr. Hall, the Commissioner, either from press of business or otherwise, is very slow. I thought at first I would go to Austin myself and see him rather than wait to hear from him by letter, but I compromised by writing to Mr. Spence, asking him to hurry Mr. Hall up.

I want to lease something over 13,000 acres, and if I succeed, I will rest easy on the ranch business for a while. I would like to know as soon as possible, so that I can look elsewhere if this fails, but if Mr. Spence is like his son Robert, I may have to go down and hurry him up. During the summer months we do not require much land, so I'm in no particular press, but working as fast as possible 'twill take me several weeks to get things in good order so that I can have time to attend to other matters more to my taste.

I believe the foregoing covers the ground somewhat as to what I *have* been doing; now what I *intend* to do, Little Girl, only one thing is such that it cannot be altered by human interference. I might change all my business plans, so far as intentions go, tomorrow. I have sold nearly 1000 sheep since two weeks ago, and might close out entirely any time.

It's a business in which it's almost impossible to have decided intentions. There are more provisos than when anticipating a ride on some Texas rail-roads. The *one* intention from which no power on earth can change me is that before many months pass by, I will call you My Little Wife.

Good-night,
Yours Affectionately,
J.B.M.

---

[1] Mollie suffered the headaches all her life. It seems probable that they were caused by her satisfying a craving for sweets. For example, while she was living in Graham after college, Judge McCormick, on each return from a session out of town, would bring her a novel and a box of candy. Her practice was to sit up all night, reading the novel and eating the chocolates. She liked to eat lettuce after sprinkling a leaf with sugar and rolling it like a tortilla.

[2] During this period, most of the land in West Texas was unclaimed range land.

30

Marienfeld, August 4, 1889

My Dear Mollie,

I do not like letters in the form of a diary myself, but your taste may differ. At any rate I'll risk it once. I feel like writing this afternoon and may not be in the mood when your letter comes, so will talk to you a little now, and some more when I hear from you. I've just finished another lonesome mid-day meal. Had the pleasure of cooking it myself, and also the enjoyment of it in solitude. It's useless to remark that I've eaten Sunday dinners which I appreciated more.

I guess you'll be surprised to hear that I was guilty of attending another Midland dance Friday night. I know I surprised myself. I went out to that village Friday, intending to return in the afternoon, but with one thing and another I was unable to get away until night, so stayed over until next morning.

The two oldest Mullinix girls were very anxious to go to the ball and their only chance was for me to take them. I tried to talk them out of the notion but 'twas no use. They said they never had been anywhere since leaving my protecting care, that their father was too tired to take them out at night and would not let them go with anyone else. I at last consented and we went.

I remarked to Ella, the oldest, on the way home that the Midland society folks were not so rapid as they were last February, that possibly the warm weather had something to do with it. No, she said, the Methodists had been having revival meetings and all the roughest characters had joined the church and couldn't go to dances. She wished that two more young ladies, giving their names, who were present at this ball, would join, then they would have quite a respectable crowd at the parties.

This original idea in itself amuses me, but the matter of fact tone in which she said it, as if the easiest way to rid the dances of some objectionable features was to have those who did not understand behaving themselves join the church, made it sound very laughable.

I inspected several "desirable building spots," said to be, at least, by the real estate agents, but the advantages of one piece of ground over another in a town like this are very slight. I knew perfectly well where I wanted the ground before asking anyone's advice.

A person who has been here as long as I have has it forced upon him after a while that no location is favorable on the east side or north side of the main part of any west Texas town. If we are compelled to have the south and west winds, we prefer them fresh from the prairies and not after they become loaded with sand and dust from the streets. I found two lots which suited me very well and told the agent I would take them, and also the third lot adjoining the two if he could find the owner and buy it. Three will be ¼ of a block. I suppose we can "make out" on this much room, especially when, at the present time, on one side there's not a house in sight.

I rec'd a letter from Mr. Spence yesterday, informing me that Mr. Hall would lease me the lands I wanted. So I guess the question of where our home is to be, and where the ranch is to be, after so long a time is settled. I will have to go up to the land in a day or two and survey off a few lines and find the best place to put in a water works. I don't think any one realizes the value of water until they stay on the plains awhile, either for watering stock or dampening the ground.

August 5. I came into the Post Office this afternoon, but did not get your letter. I did not intend to send this until I *did* hear from you, but as I expect to go away tomorrow for two or three days and this being already written, it's not worth while, I guess, to keep you waiting.

It's my intention now to call on you when I get back from survey-ing. Unless I am detained, I may get off Friday morning and be with you Saturday night. If I don't get started on that day 'twill be Monday night before we can have an interview. I am not *always* as promptly on time as I was when I went to see you before, and when I say it's uncer-tain about my arrival, you must not be disappointed if I fail to "show up." I will write you if I do not get away Friday. Tell Cousin Lou that I will board with her again for a few days if she will let me.

My time is limited, and I do not owe you a letter anyway. I guess you'd better answer this. I may have time to get your letter, and if I do not I will find it waiting for me after my visit

Yours Affectionately,

J.B.M.

Your father hasn't written me yet; but I'm not nearly so impatient for his reply as I am always for yours.

J.

NOTE: *J.B.M.'s happy frame of mind is, however, to suffer a setback when he does receive a reply from Mollie's father.*

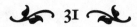

31

Weatherford, Texas, Aug. 9, 1889
[To the] Hon. A.P. McCormick
Waukesha, Wis.

Dear Sir:

That your letter recently received both surprised and pained me I need scarcely say. I exceedingly regret that my unfortunate use of certain language caused you to place a construction on my letter to you entirely different from that which was intended. 'Twas not a feeling of self importance that led me to make the remark about not asking advice.

You are to a certain extent acquainted with my family affairs and the out-lines of my own history. You realize how completely I stand alone, and have stood alone for years as regards anyone to whom I *could* go for counsel. Depending altogether on my own resources, without any education of a practical nature, I've been forced by necessity rather than otherwise to act on my own responsibility. I used the expression in commencing my letter, casually and without any idea or intention that it would be considered conceited or disrespectful. I know you would not intentionally do any one an injustice, so this explanation is necessary.

I appreciate your good opinion very highly myself, and if this were not so, I know 'twould not add any to Mollie's peace of mind for me to cause any unpleasantness between you and her. I regret that my letter gave you the impression that 'twas mere formality my asking your approval of our plans.

I suppose my hopes that I can make her happy rest on the same basis upon which such hopes usually rest in similar cases. My affection for her is as great as a man's could possibly be for a woman, and I have her word for it that she has a high regard for me. My sole object hereafter will be to provide for her needs and study her desires. I can give her a comfortable home, and if unforeseen disasters do not occur, can keep it so.

My business depends on so many influences that one cannot accurately say what a year's returns will be, but with my present number of sheep something over four thousand, I should say we can safely rely on from twelve hundred to two thousand dollars per year for household expenses. Of my standing financially in the community in which I live, I will simply say that my notes are generally considered good in the banks. If you would like me to write you any more fully in regard to business affairs I will do so with pleasure.

If there is anything in this letter of which you do not approve, please attribute it to my ignorance of compositions of this character and give me the credit of trying, at least, not to displease you a second time.

Your letter to me was somewhat delayed and reached me on the eve of my departure for a visit to Graham. This is the first opportunity I've had for replying. I expect to go to Graham tomorrow, and will be there three or four days. Any letters you write me, please direct to Marienfeld, Martin Co.

Yours Truly,
J. B. McGill

Weatherford, Texas, Aug. 16, 1889

Dear Little Sweetheart,

As I have never yet been able to resist the temptation of writing to you the first opportunity after telling you good-bye, I guess it's not worth while to bring an ineffectual struggle against the desire to have a talk with you tonight, especially when I flatter myself that you would be disappointed did you fail to get this letter *tomorrow* night. I know you do not expect anything except a repetition of such things as my letters have been filled with heretofore, consequently I will not strain my imagination any by endeavoring to *think*.

I do not mean that you are so far carried away with your love for me (altho' I know you like me pretty well now), that a letter filled with expressions of my affection for you is all you desire, but you have learned by this time that with rare exceptions my epistles contain little else, so when you begin to read one you do not anticipate much change.

Your hopes that my trip here, so far as the weather was concerned, would be pleasant, were realized. The sun did not shine but very little until late in the evening and the day was all that could have been desired. The same number of miles and the same number of rocks, I need scarcely say, still lie between here and Graham.

Mr. Thompson, the hotel man, seemed very glad to see me, but I attribute his happiness to the fact that last Saturday I went off without paying my bill, and so do not feel flattered by his kind reception.

The stage-driver was inclined to be curious, so I satisfied him to a moderate extent, and requested him to keep silent towards others. Don't think I'm one who confides in all he meets (but you know I do not, of course), but I thought very likely the driver would do more talking in a speculative way than he would otherwise. I may be wrong but I do not think so.

I'm terribly home-sick tonight, and it's not yet twenty-four hours since I saw you. How I'm to get through the time until I see you again I cannot say. There is one consolation. I guess I've told you good-bye for the last time when expecting to be separated for any length of time, and when I again stop in Weatherford on my way west, I will not be home-sick nor lonely.* I will have the only thing that makes a home attractive with me. The only person in all the world who can make me happy, or unhappy as she wills, will be my companion.

So long as we both shall live, when you are in one place and I in another I will be homesick, when we are together, no matter where the spot be on which we stand, I can take your hand in mine and feel that there is home. This is figurative, of course. If we happened to be lost on the prairie some cold night, or placed in any equally unpleasant situation, I expect we'd both feel a slight touch of the above mentioned complaint.

I tried to crowd enough of your society and the happiness which it ever brings into the last five days to "sorter" bridge over the weeks which will pass before I see you again. But I had as well try to eat enough, in the same number of days, to sustain life during the next two months or more, as to imagine this could be done.

These few lines may give you the impression that I have the "blues," but I think this is not the case exactly. In one sense I feel perfectly contented. Looking forward the future promises all the happiness I could wish, but, my "Darling Old Gal," I wish you were as near me now as you were this time last night.

I'm very, very sleepy and if you have any trouble in reading the foregoing 'twill be for *this* reason and the various changes of the electric light. If this epistle proves short, please do not retaliate but return good for evil, and write me a nice long one Sunday.

With more love than many women ever receive, I will say, My Dear Little Girl, good-night.

Yours Affectionately,
J.B.M.

* In spite of her father's attitude, Mollie and J.B.M. are planning to marry early in November.

33

Marienfeld, Aug. 18, 1889

My Dear Little Girl,

If it were not that I shall have very little time for letter writing during the next few days, I would wait until a more favorable opportunity before trying to compose an epistle to you.

The train brought me to my destination on time last night, 10:30 p.m., and I discovered that I was somewhat tired. My comfort was not added to by the fact that nearly all day I had been afflicted with the headache. . . .

It had entirely passed away this morning, but I was still feeling rather gloomy both mentally and physically until the Post Office opened and I rec'd my mail which had been accumulating during the last ten days. My mental gloom was dispelled by the letter from you written on the 7th. . . .

I found my Post Office box well filled with communications of a business nature written several days ago, and requesting my presence in different localities, so my *physical* gloom was *necessarily* dispelled. A postal card from Mullinix asking me to come to Midland about our town lots; a note from the man who is to dig the well on the new ranch wanting me up there. I hope my horses are well rested, because they will get some exercise for the next few days.

The expected letter from your father was not among them. Of course, I cannot say what effect it might have had on my spirits, whether elevating or depressing.

I have seen no one from the ranch yet, and do not know how things are progressing. I was in hopes some one would come in and save me the walk. Very likely I will find a few days work there to be done. It's generally the case when I've been absent.

I had a note from Mr. Spence sending me the lease-contract for the ranch land, but a slight error necessitates its being sent back for correction. A card from Mr. Dumble asking the date on which his note was due. I suppose he intends to settle. I wish you were with me so that when my mail came in I could give it to you to read. 'Twould be more satisfactory than this way. But then I wish you were with me for so many reasons that it's hardly worth while to mention any *one*.

I learn the Methodist minister from Big Springs has been holding protracted meetings here last week, but where his congregation came from I'm unable to say. Sometime ago he had a falling out with the Marienfelders and quit coming here to preach at all. The people are always liberal in their contributions, but one Sunday he was not exactly satisfied, and said if they wanted him to preach they must pay his passage to and from Big Springs and furnish him a pleasant stopping place while here. As it was a matter of indifference to the majority whether he came or not, they failed to respond.

I suppose his conscience troubled him that such a heathenish place should be so near him, so last week he came up, rented a vacant house on his own responsibility, and constructed seats out of rough boards placed on boxes. He was offered the courthouse free of charge, and which has comfortable seats, but he gave several reasons for not accepting, the principal one being that the place he had chosen would not cost the people here anything, hence my ignorance of where he found his congregation.

According to a theory of that admirable sister of yours, Cousin Lucy, the best letters are those which do not contain any news, or at least do not confine themselves to news. If your tastes are the same, then many of my letters heretofore will prove of more interest than this one, but my "poetic nature" is not in the ascendancy just now, so I've had to confine myself to prose. Believing, as I do now, that our regard for each other is getting to be more evenly balanced, I can judge you by myself with more certainty of being correct than ever before. Consequently, our letters to each other will always be interesting, and their arrival more eagerly awaited than anything the mails ever brought us, or ever will bring. Am I right, Sweetheart?

Remember me, with regards, to your sisters.

Yours Affectionately,
J.B.M.

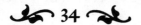 34

Marienfeld, Aug. 28, 1889

My Dear Little Girl,

I'm feeling in a better humor tonight than when I wrote you last, and as something may happen to put me out again before a great while, I guess I'd better give you the benefit of my good nature while this spell is on me. Especially as I feel like talking to you a little.

I went out to Midland this morning and spent most of the day in that city, returning to the ranch here in time for a late supper.

I will be thankful when I get my various enterprises in this section somewhat more concentrated. A young fellow asked me today what I was doing with myself. I told him I was struggling with three different "outfits" located in a triangular shape several miles apart, two flocks of sheep near Marienfeld, digging a well thirty miles north, and building a house in Midland. I failed to mention the most important one, that I had a little girl who occupied my spare moments located still farther away in another direction. I guess tho', this fact is pretty well known by this time. My building a house is enough to create the impression that *some* change is going to occur.

My present happy frame of mind is occasioned principally by being relieved of a pressure of a financial nature. Nothing serious, but I was somewhat bothered about some notes I owed the bank. I called on the banker today and told him 'twould save me an immense amount of speculation if he would grant me leave of absence, about the time my note came due, for a thousand dollars of the amount. He said certainly he could, so I feel easy. I could "pay up" well enough after shearing, from wool proceeds, but will be out some expense on the new ranch, and our house, and did not like to sell any more sheep at present.

Now I want to ask you a very important question which I neglected asking when I was with you. Do you want the house near the street or back in the yard? Would you like it near the side street or some distance from it? If you could see the place at the present writing, you'd think such questions absurd, because 'twould take an engineer to say where the streets were, but the time may come when these things will change, and it just as well be built where you like. If I had any preference in the matter, I would gladly give way to yours, and as I have not, you need have no fears about saying exactly what will please you best. . . .

Aug. 29th. When I came back from Graham the last time the first thing I did was to order some El Paso grapes, which you remember I promised to send you. When they came I discovered they were entirely too ripe to send such a distance, and that the season for them had so far advanced 'twould not be possible to get any to you this year in respectable shape. I hope tho' that in other ways I can make you happy enough to enable you to wait until next August for the grapes, when you'll likely be nearer the vines. I need scarcely say that the basket I intended for you was eaten mostly by myself, acting as your agent, and I expect in this case the agent accomplished more than the principal would have done. . . .

You know that you have a power over me that a woman seldom has over a man, and I could see very plainly when I was with you the last time that you rather enjoyed it than otherwise. I expect it is somewhat flattering to a woman's vanity that she can say to "one man come and he cometh" and to the same one "go and he goeth" and that her commands are obeyed all out of love for her. The consolation to the man, however, is not much different when he knows he is loved too well to be ordered to do anything very difficult.

I used to often wonder if a man and his wife did not sometimes grow tired of each other. It seemed to me that day after day and year after year their society would grow a trifle monotonous. This has ceased to appear strange. The opposite is the curious part, how a man can *compel* himself to stay even for a limited time away from the woman he loves. I never want to engage in any undertaking which will keep me apart from you very long.

I expect your next letter tomorrow and trust I will not be disappointed.

> *Yours Aff* —
> J.B.M.

Later. If I was feeling good before I came in town you can imagine how much better I feel since reading your first "love" letter. I wouldn't have called it by that name, however, myself. If you wish to know what *my* private opinion is of those who expressed their sentiments last Sunday, I will simply say they have very poor taste, and I should dislike to have them judge for me in similar cases. I, of course, do not mean to say that I do not appreciate having a girl like Cousin Sallie for a cousin or sister, but I rather think you are right when you say she would not have occupied much of my attention when *you* were in the neighborhood. I had seen Cousin Sallie more than I had you until last winter and I know full well I would always say good-bye without any very serious thoughts forcing themselves upon me.

You don't know how much I appreciate your writing without waiting to hear from me, and as my long silence was fully explained in my last letter you are over your anger by this time. . . .

Once more I will tell you farewell with regards to all.

Yrs. Aff.

J.

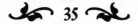

Marienfeld, Texas, Aug. 31st, 1889.

My Dear Little Girl,

. . . I had quite a long talk with a young fellow the night after the Midland barbecue on the subject of girls, and surprised even myself with the amount of advice I was able to give him on how to make a woman care for one. We had both been up to the dance, and each growing tired looking on, had walked down town. He expressed some thought to the effect that he would be just as well off if he were dead, and this, with other remarks, made me guess that a woman was at the "bottom of it."

I finally told him I thought such was the case, and as he neither denied nor affirmed it, I became pretty well convinced that I was right. If you could have heard me telling him what to do in such cases, growing quite eloquent (or loud) at times, you'd have thought I had made this a study of years instead of months, and that my experience had not been confined to one woman.

I guess all I told him, however, in more than an hour's talk, could be put in a very few words. Simply love her enough. If you don't love her enough at first, go away for a while, love her when you are away, don't count the cost of postage stamps in telling her so, return and love her more than ever. If she doesn't think too much of some other fellow beforehand, she will in the end love you. I expect, tho' my experience *has* only been with you, that I was not very far wrong.

I might have also told him, if it hadn't sounded like talking sentiment to a man, that when your girl *does* let you know she loves you just a little, 'twill be the most successful moment of your life, and up to that time the happiest, altho' many *happier* days will come after. All the desponding, and longing-for-death moments thru' which you have recently passed will fade away. One *loving* look from the eyes of the woman *you* love will repay you for months of anxiety.

I know quite well, however, that I cannot always judge others by myself, either in this or other things. It's a mystery to me, whenever I think of it, how your Cousin Frank can accept the present situation and remind himself continually of what he has lost. If his position and mine were reversed I do not think 'twould make my loss any lighter or easier to bear by being near you.

He may possibly have the same views of you that you had of yourself, that after becoming better acquainted, he will not love you so well. I believe you made this remark to me along with another, that you had no affection in your composition, both of them as far wrong as was mine about the ice berg. If this is his idea, my advice would be not to place too great faith in it. I know full well the last time I was with you I thought you more desirable, attractive, admirable, or more something, which I lack a word to express, if such a thing were possible, than ever before.

I guess unless your father positively refuses us the use of his parlor for a few minutes, we need have no fears about arranging our affairs. Of course, it's only been for your sake all the time that I cared the slightest. I'm under the impression somehow that I have more influence among my homefolks than you have among yours. I will venture the assertion that even Aunt Em will be glad to see both of us if we should ever call on her. I wish tho' yours did not have the power to make things unpleasant for you any more than mine does for me. In a short time I guess they won't.

Goodbye,
Yours Affectionately,
J.B.M.

36

Marienfeld, Sept. 4th, 1889

Dear Little Sweetheart,

I don't know whether you or the mails are the cause of my not getting a letter this morning, but I know I was very much disappointed. I *would* wait until your letter *did* come if I did not have to leave tomorrow morning, and cannot get it before Friday or Saturday. Then *you'd* be disappointed, and it won't do for us both to be in this state at once.

I needed one today more than usual. I've been "bothered" a good-deal lately, and find myself depending considerably on the consolation afforded by the thought that the affection of one dear little girl is worth everything else. I believe if it were not for this I'd be inclined to have the "blues" sometimes. I've been in the habit always of looking on the bright side of everything. Consequently, this complaint effects me very seldom. If I could commence now and do everything myself which I want done, very likely I would not grow impatient.

I went out to where the well machine was at work, last Sunday. Possibly 'twas a punishment for going on Sunday, that I've had no better "luck." I found a hole had been dug sixty feet ending in a bed of clay. The most discouraging thing known to well diggers or persons needing water, is to meet with a result like the above. With rare exceptions no hole has been dug deep enough in this country to penetrate the clay, and no water is ever found in it. So I've lost several days time, besides the expense of this hole and the prospect staring me in the face of meeting with no better success in another place. Then too, I will need water in a very short time, and as we say on the plains, "need it bad." I've always been so fortunate in digging wells, never failing to get plenty of water, that I never had any idea I would miss it this time.

If I go on in this strain much longer, you *will* think I'm low-spirited, or something similar, but I'm "keeping up" pretty well. I've got to make another trip up there tomorrow, and look over the land a little more. I think there is already a well on one part of it. If this proves to be the case, I will not make any more attempts at digging myself until later on.

I will need all the patience I can command for the next week. I expect to commence shearing in a few days, and if there is one thing more than another in this business calculated to try "men's souls," 'tis overseeing a crowd of fifteen or twenty Mexicans. 'Twill not last long, however.

When I wrote the above I had forgotten the fact that I have to sit on the jury at the next term of court, next Monday week. *This* is equally as trying. I had some hopes of claiming Midland as my place of residence before court met, but it's too late now. There are hardly enough men *in* Martin County to make a jury, so twice a year I have this honor thrust upon me. . . .

I wish I'd had your letter today. I will feel lonesome now until I come back again. I expect you'll think it "silly!" but I always carry your last letter with me until the next one comes. The one in my pocket now is dated Aug. 28th. I'll convince you after awhile, possibly, how much you are to me. I don't think you fully realize it even yet.

Affectionately Yours,

J.B.M.

III

Dear
Little Sweetheart

37

Marienfeld, Sept. 6, 1889

My Dear Little Girl,

I guess your letter just rec'd is already answered, but then, you are such a dear little sweetheart, and write a fellow such nice letters, and I love you so well, that I will answer it again. I came into the ranch late this evening and altho' I'd been riding since early this morning, I went out and caught a fresh horse, and made a trip to the Post Office, feeling fully repaid for the ride by the receipt of your letter.

I used to love to write to you, even when I thought you might answer from a sense of duty, or through politeness, so it's not strange that now the pleasure of writing is much greater, when I know no such things influence you. I expect you will think, if you do not say it, that you've heard something of this kind before, but then I know you'll make an exception in my favor, and not judge me as you do the unfortunate young man who called upon you the other night. I wish I was near enough to you at the present moment to love you a little, *right.* I guess I'd not make many quotations from the by-gone men of poetic fame, but I think you said you preferred originality in love, and not the kind made perfect by long practice. I think with a very slight acquaintance with you, I could learn that if a fellow tried to make himself entertaining by saying sweet things, you'd soon prefer ''his room to his company.''

I think it very likely that if things had been ordered differently, and we had not been thrown together last winter, while both of us might have settled down and lived happily in the married state, neither would have ever felt the complete satisfaction in our love for our life partners as we do for each other. I know *I* feel this way, and altho' it's awful hard to get you to *admit* anything like this, I *know* you love me better than you ever would any one else. I expect it sounds conceited, but I guess you would have gone thru' life, deluded with the idea that love was imaginary, and sentiment silly, if I hadn't been so ''set'' on ''having my own way.''

As you have already told me, and showed me, that having my own way in this one matter had made you happy, I don't think you ought to write of it as a *failing*. I guess if we live together until we reach the limit of old age, you will never find me again trying so persistently to influence you, and I don't think *I* will ever find *you* so hard to influence.

I remember Mullinix and I were once talking about the best way for two men to get along together smoothly. I said each one should make up his mind at the start to always give way to the other. He said, yes, and afterwards each one will *think* he himself has always given way.

I think frequently, tho', that in the case of a man and his wife, the reverse of this is seen. The wife gets so much into her husband's ways, that she *thinks* she is having her own will when really she is carrying out his desires. While I do not care for you and I to indulge in every day quarrels, I don't know that I'm particularly desirous of your becoming my counterpart. I'm a selfish man, but I try not to be one, and I have too great respect for your mental powers, to wish to always act as your guide.

This ranch is like a young Mexico tonight, some twenty-two or three inhabitants of that country being on hand. They are all inveterate gamblers, and every evening they spread a blanket on the ground and indulge in the Mexican game of "monte," betting off the "checks" we give them in keeping tally of the number of sheep each one shears. Each one of these checks is worth four cents or five cents, whatever we pay for shearing. I have very frequently paid to *half* of the men nearly all the money due them *all*, while the other half had the pleasure (!) of working for nothing.

I think they try to eat enough while shearing lasts to do them until the next season. I was telling Cousin Lou that in running a sheep ranch, a person's provision bill would amount to so much, that they could take out the provisions used for a small family, and not know the difference. If she were to see what this crowd consumes, my assertion would be credited. In the matter of meat, they eat two sheep every day, [with] everything else in proportion. It's lucky they don't stay longer in one place.

Sheep shearing, Colfax County, New Mexico. Courtesy Museum of New Mexico, negative number 57885.

It's growing late and I've been on the go since daylight. My lamp is *not* trimmed and is burning very dimly, with a smoked chimney. My eyes are getting tired. I'm sleepy, and as your letter was answered before it came, I expect I'd better say farewell.

Yours Affectionately,

J.B.M.

38

Marienfeld, Sept. 9, 1889

Dear Little Girl,

I'm writing under difficulties tonight and I believe I'm about the only fellow in this country who would try to write to his girl when the surroundings are so much against it. A very narrow window sill forms my table, and you know this is not the best place in the world for writing. As this letter will be a day late anyway, and for once I am under the necessity of answering two letters in one, I will not make you wait until a more favorable opportunity. It's not worth while, hardly, to tell you how much I appreciated getting two nice letters from you at the same time.

If I can or do make you as happy as you can and do make me, then I guess we'll manage to enjoy life pretty thoroughly without the assistance of anyone else. I need you with me, Little Girl, every day. I guess tho', if you were around tonight, and the situation the same, you'd feel somewhat lost. What I mean, however, is that 'twould be very pleasant to have you close by, so I could forget for a while, in talking to you, the trials and tribulations which hover over a man during his walk thro' life. . . .

It's rather hard on a fellow, too, to be as far from his girl as I am, and know that other fellows can go to see her three times a week or oftener. If a letter from me, however, can cause you to show in your countenance that you are made happy by its receipt, then I should not complain because the other fellow enjoys your society only for a short time. I expect you'll begin to think if I continue to write in this way about your cousin Frank, that I do not like for him to see you so much, but truly I do not mean to convey any such impression. You learned I expect, at the beginning of our acquaintance, that I am generally outspoken and do not waste much time in hinting. If you did anything I did not like I expect you'd be requested to change, and not hinted at in an obscure manner. . . .

The Mexican picnic is still in session at this ranch, but if the weather continues good, I will turn it over to someone else the day after tomorrow. So far things have progressed smoothly. The cook went on a strike today and I did not blame him much. I think his boarders now number about thirty, and he said he could not cook for such a crowd. I agreed to raise his wages, but he gave up the job, and I put *two* new ones at it. If it were my first experience, very likely I would be worried considerably, but I understand the Mexican nature pretty well by this time, and do not have much trouble.

I remember the first time I had Mexicans to do the shearing. I hardly knew before the work was done whether they or I owned the ranch. Most of these men have worked for me several times before, and they have gradually been convinced that they are only hired hands. All things considered, the Mexicans are preferable to white men for work of this kind.

I expect you think there is some kind of falling off in my letters to you. It seems to me sometimes that such is the case. I know, as far as mere composition went, I could write you better letters heretofore than I can now. One reason, I guess, up to the time I made my first visit to you, I had nothing whatever on my mind but *you*, and since then the only object I've had in view was to make you happy.

I suppose since I've been successful in "having my own way" in that direction, the necessity for being poetically eloquent and irresistibly persuasive has disappeared, and my mind is more on other matters. I can't account for it any other way. I know so far as *thinking* goes, if my thoughts for a moment get on to any other subject, *that* subject, be it ever so remote, will lead to some other until the chain is completed, which leads back to you.

As to this particular letter, I will make the same excuse as did the last preacher I heard in Marienfeld. He says, "Our light is bad and we have sand in our eyes, so if we make any mistakes in reading the gospel, we hope you will excuse us." I might also add my oft repeated excuse that I'm sleepy.

Goodnight, My Little Girl,
Yours Aff.
J.B.M.

I had *two* letters of yours in my pocket when I went to the P.O. today so can very easily carry the other two in their stead. I guess if this thing continues much longer, I will have to carry *three* around with me.

 39

Marienfeld, Sept. 13, 1889

My Dear Little Girl,

This is going to be another complaining letter. I couldn't write any other kind tonight, and is likely to be short, because I'm considerably tired. I started off this morning disappointed in not getting a letter from you, but as very likely the fault was not yours I shall not complain *at* you. If you will kindly ask your friend, Mr. Parker, to send letters addressed to me by Weatherford instead of Henrietta, I will receive them one day sooner and thereby be saved numerous disappointments, and you will not be accused so frequently of not writing.

I bid farewell to the Mexican shearers yesterday. This fact alone should render me happy for the next eight months when the season comes around again, but it doesn't. I'm not only bothered now but worried, and tonight physically tired.

You remember I told you I was the owner of a house in this city, which for various reasons I intended moving to Midland. Well, several days ago, I had a carpenter to take it down and engaged another man to load it on the car [wagon]. The other man, like many of his fellow citizens, is slow, so when I came in town this morning, nothing had been done. The lumber was lying in a confused heap on the ground originally occupied by the house.

I was reminded very forcibly of the lesson we used to read in our first or second reader about the lark building her nest in the field of grain, not thinking it necessary to move so long as the farmer depended on hired help to cut the wheat. I thought to myself that if any bird had

Sheep shearing camp, near Socorro, New Mexico, 1902. Courtesy Museum of New Mexico, negative number 142641.

made its nest around that lumber pile, 'twould be a good idea to follow the lark's example in the latter act, because I intended to do as the farmer did, and perform the work myself, or at least take a prominent part of it.

The first thing necessary was to take all the nails out of the planks, and thusly have I been occupied all day. I have managed to get some very respectable blisters on my hands, and make myself, as I said, tired. To make matters worse, several of the Marienfeld idlers were continually around making comments. I hate to do work of this kind that any one could do, when I have so much else on hand, but I guess I will see it through with tomorrow. I wish many times every day, that I could do *everything* myself. As it is I can't do *any*thing except wait on other people.

I've been trying to get rid of all the sheep, and may succeed. If this happens, I will not attempt anything more in the business way until you and I are comfortably settled. As things are now, they take all my time. Unless I get the new ranch supplied with water very soon, the out-look is not promising. I don't know what success the well diggers are having since I left there a week ago.

I told you I was something of a fatalist in the way things moved along. I would like now to know *why* everything seems to combine to "set me back" in my efforts to get affairs running smoothly by the time *you* are ready for our wedding. I fail to understand it. Never in all my experience have I met with anything which I was inclined to call "bad luck" before.

There has hardly been a time for the last three or four years when in a few weeks time I could not have arranged everything in good shape and gone after you, brought you home, and never been bothered at all.

I have known all along that I was going to be crowded somewhat financially. I was not rendered any easier the other day by receiving a letter from the Lampasas Bank that Mr. Dumble's note had been protested for non-payment. This made me, to put it mildly, mad. I had no use for the money at the time 'twas loaned, but now I need it. Even if I were fully able, I would seriously object to paying another man's extravagant wedding expenses.

You began one of your letters the other day by saying I no doubt thought you a snare, delusion, etc. I wonder if the surroundings at present indicate in any way that the time will come when *you'll* think in sober earnest that *I'm* one. As you well know, lack of confidence in my ability to succeed in undertakings has never been one of my failings. I've frequently expressed my opinion of others, who seemed to be afraid to do anything for themselves, but were waiting for "something to turn up." While I do not know that I am losing that confidence, still, when a person comes up suddenly "against a wall" in any direction he may turn, it certainly grows discouraging. Altho' I've learned long ago that

it's very seldom anything *does* "turn up" it would help me along won-
derfully if the sun, figuratively speaking, would break thro' the clouds
in an unexpected place.

It would be awful hard on me, Little Girl, if the time *should* come
when you'd think you had made a mistake, but as providence has been
kind so far in causing you to care for me, we will hope that such a punishment is not in store for either of us.

I guess I will go out to Midland tomorrow, if I get thro' with my job
here in time. I certainly will hear from you in the morning, and may add
a few more lines. For the present, as I am writing in the school-teacher's
room, and I think it's near his bed time, I will say good-night.

Don't you feel blue, now, because I'm a little that way.

Yours Aff.
J.B.M.

I was disappointed again this morning in not hearing from you, but was
to some extent comforted by receiving an offer from a publishing company wishing me to act as a book agent. If you don't hurry up and write
I may accept. I don't know of any punishment I could inflict which
would worry you so much as to be engaged to one of these beings.

Yours
J.

Marienfeld, Sept. 17, 1889

My Dear Little Sweetheart,
Do you realize the fact that you are treating me in a very unbecom-
ing manner? Do you know that the last letter I had from you was dated
Sept. 4th? Do you know this is the third letter I have written you since

receiving your last? Do you remember that I told you besides being disappointed, I could not help feeling uneasy when you were silent beyond a reasonable time?

All these questions being answered in the affirmative, allow me to ask why you are behaving in such a way? I could write with much more satisfaction tonight, if I had heard from you recently. As it is, you will have to "make out" with a one-sided letter again.

I finished up with the jury business this afternoon, and trust it will be my last appearance in the Court room of Martin County. I occupied the exalted (!) position of foreman of the grand jury, but this did not help to make the last two days less monotonous. Examining witnesses in regard to crimes committed is not a very attractive past-time.

I've seen a case today which has caused me to do some more thinking over the strange way things are ordered, or *happen* without being ordered. Some months ago, a man in one of the north west counties shot at another. He was arrested and put in jail here, but released on bond. He should have been tried at this term of court, but several members of the grand jury being pretty well convinced that he was insane, a doctor was sent for who expressed the same opinion. So instead of finding a bill of indictment the *County* Judge was directed to have him tried for insanity, and sent to the asylum.

This evening the first thing I heard after leaving the courthouse was that this man was supposed to be dying. I went down to a small outhouse to which he had been taken, and found him surrounded by quite a crowd, with a physician and several other men doing all they could to counteract the effects of a dose of strychnine, which the doctor said he must have taken.

Now comes the part which puzzles me. Why is it so hard for a crowd of men to see a man *die*, that they cannot help trying to prevent it? I do not think that among them all, there was *one* to whom his living or dying would have made the slightest difference, yet if he had been a brother to those trying to save him, they could not have made greater efforts.

This is not all. Would he not have been better off dead? If he lives

(I left town before the thing was ended), he will in all probability end his days in a lunatic asylum.

Another thing [is] hard to understand. Why does an overruling providence *allow* such a "throwing away" of life, health, and strength as seem to be thrown away here? He was or is a powerful man physically, and one could easily see that death would have no easy victory, yet thousands of people who love life, who are loved by their friends, and occupying places in the world hard to fill, must die for want of that which *this* man was throwing away.

One other feature of the case would have been hard for me to realize a short time ago, but is different now. The whole history of this part of the man's life dates back only to where he began to love a woman. The man whom he tried to kill was his rival. It might be called insanity, but I *know* perfectly well now, when I trust I'm in my right mind, that if such an impossible thing should come to pass that some other man should come between you and me, I would not care to live and see it, nor would I care to have the other fellow enjoy his triumph.

There is such a thing as a man loving a woman too much for perfect happiness, in one way only. That is on account of a feeling of uneasiness. I've frequently mentioned this to you before, and I feel it now by not hearing from you in so long.

I had for a companion on my ride to Midland last Saturday, an elderly gentleman from down near San Antonio, who was here on some land business in the court. He asked me some questions which led me to tell him I was going to be married. Then he made the following curious assertion. He says, "If you are *happily* married you will be a very unfortunate man." On my asking an explanation, he said if a man loved his wife to such an extent that she was *everything* to him, a feeling of something going to happen would be so ever-present that he would always be uneasy.

I soon was certain he was giving me his own experience, and finally asked him if he thought he would have been better off if he had *never* married. He says, "No, my wife and I are very happy even if I do have this feeling when I'm away from her."

So I guess, My Little Girl, I will change the old saying somewhat and say, "'Tis better to have loved 'too well' than ne'er to have loved at all."*

Yours Aff,
J.B. McGill

* "'Tis better to have loved and lost/Than never to have loved at all." Alfred, Lord Tennyson, *In Memoriam*.

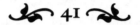

41

Marienfeld, Sept. 22, 1889

My Dear Little Girl,

. . . I went out to Midland the day I mailed my last letter to you, and just returned this evening. It being Sunday, I knew I couldn't get in the Post Office, and hadn't any idea I'd be fortunate enough to get your letter or letters before tomorrow. I asked one of the fellows at the ranch if he had brought out my mail *yesterday*, and if my countenance is as expressive as yours, any looker on could have made very accurate guesses as to whether I was happy or not when he gave me *two* from you.

My having to wait so long has demonstrated another fact. No matter what worries I may have on the outside, a *little* uneasiness about you takes every thing else out of my mind. A relief from *this* uneasiness makes me contented again even if the other surroundings are unchanged. Consequently I'm much happier now than when I wrote either the last time or the time before.

Other things are not quite so depressing as when I composed that forlorn epistle to you ending with the threat to become a book-agent, but I do not regret writing it. It called forth such a nice reply, I feel

Sandstorm over Midland, Texas, February 20, 1894. The McGill home may have resembled the house in the picture. Courtesy Midland County Historical Museum.

tempted to repeat it just for the sake of reading again your expressions of confidence in me. It makes a fellow "feel good" just to *read* such things. When I have you near me all the time to *say* them, how much better 'twill be. . . .

The well-diggers were more fortunate in their second attempt and think plenty of water has been found. I will have a wind-mill up in a few days and very likely move the sheep there within the next ten days. I haven't been there myself for more than two weeks, but will have to go Tuesday, I expect. When the sheep leave here I can concentrate my energies on *two* places, Midland and the ranch. When I get the *ranch* "fixed up to my notion" I will not have to go *there* often.

Making due allowances for slowness, I think 'twill be the 20th of October before our new house will be in anything like readiness. I told the carpenter this morning I wanted two rooms of it fixed up comfortably as soon as possible, and I would lock up the others for the present. To show you how difficult it is to do anything out here, I had to send to Fort Worth for the grates for the fire-place. I will have to send somewhere else, I don't know [where] yet, for bricks for the chimney. The carpenter said this morning he expected St. Louis would have to supply the small rollers which the weights for the windows must have. It's almost impossible to get things together. I guess, tho', we'll be happy, notwithstanding these little preliminary difficulties.

I wish I had time to run down and see you. It seems a long, long time since I told you good-bye. Still it's only a little more than a month. I wonder if you think as often of me as I do of you. If you do, then you must not appear to a very good advantage when you are entertaining your callers. I know I frequently find my thoughts wandering when listening to every day conversations.

I'm not through talking to you yet, but I'll have to quit. I'm interrupted by some visitors, and think very likely I can prevail on one of them to mail this letter today. Otherwise, 'twill be one day longer in reaching you. I know it's a poor answer for *two* letters, but I will write you again before many days.

Good-bye
Yours Aff.
J.B.M.

Marienfeld, Sept. 30, 1889

My Dear Little Girl,

If I thought you believed what you said in beginning your last letter, I should feel considerably worried over it, especially at this time. But I know you don't think that I consider it either a trouble, duty, nor a "disagreeable job" to write to you, altho' I have now again to answer two letters in one. Very likely, too, this answer would help to convince you, if you had the slightest faith in the truth of your assertion, because if I ever felt less like writing in my life than I do now, I fail to recall to mind the time.

Now the reason for your having to wait so long for a letter. As I told you in my last, I expected to go up to the ranch last Tuesday, but did not suppose at the time I wrote I would be gone more than a day or two. I haven't seen a house, consequently, nor a Post Office *since* Tuesday, so you have my excuse.

I left the well diggers' camp last night after dark and reached the ranch here *sometime* this morning. It's about thirty miles up there. I, as usual, found the workmen needing assistance, and stayed as long as I did to try to render it. When I came away last night, I had lost all faith in the well being a success, but the men thought possibly it could be made one.

If I had all the "up-hill" pulls over which I've passed during my earthly career concentrated into a few weeks, I think the "hard places" would all appear easy when compared to the present out-look. I've simply come to a place where I not only can't *see* ahead, but have lost the power to *think* of a way around it. I'm not saying this to try to get you to say something "soft," but you don't believe *this* assertion you made either, so it's useless for me to have said I did not write it with that object in view. . . .

Your remarks, in one of your letters rec'd today about having my views about everything, agree with my ideas exactly. I've often intended to tell you that I like you so much better than I do myself, figuratively, literally, mentally, and spiritually, that I do not desire to pull you down to my level. I'm not sarcastic. I want you to be *yourself always* and not *my second*-self. I guess we'll both try not to *dis*agree just for the sake of argument, but I don't want you to ever think wrong is right just to please me. . . .

You need not have apologized for using pencil. I've been often tempted to do likewise even when pen and ink were just as convenient. I think you and I *ought* to be, by this time, well enough acquainted to dispense with *all* formality. I feel this way toward you, at least. I know I frequently send you letters the general appearance of which I would not care to have outsiders criticize, and if you had written to me any time in the past when you did not, just because *everything* was not favorable, I would have been saved several disappointments.

I have had so much more to bother me lately, that unless I'm reminded of the fact by you, I seldom think of your father's disapproval of our plans. This does not sound very complimentary to *him*, but it may relieve your fears in regard to my being critical. The only thing which troubles me at all in the matter is whether he will try to make things unpleasant for you before you come to your new home. This fact worries me more than all else, for you to be made unhappy even for a little while on my account, when it seems utterly impossible for me to prevent it.

I made arrangements for our house when I first came back from Graham in July. When I make a contract with a man I like to keep my part of it. But for this I could have found some carpenter not so busy as the one who is to build it, and could have had every thing in readiness by now. I know, if this were any consolation to me, that I'm bothered more than you. One other fact which *is* a consolation, is that *you are* not blaming and *will* not blame *me* for the present surroundings.

I feel somewhat better since I began writing. I often find this to be the case when I talk to you.

Yours Aff.
J.B.M.

❧ 43 ❧

Marienfeld, Oct. 2, 1889

My Dear Little Girl,

. . . If my memory is not at fault, I believe I reach the advanced age of 33 today, but it's been so long since anything unusual has occurred on this day I hardly take any notice of my birthdays.

I've heard it said that if a person works pretty hard on the anniversary day of their advent into this world, it's a good sign they will be kept busy during the next year. If such be the case then I guess I'll not be idle much for the coming twelve months. I've been engaged nearly all day in the occupation of helping load and unload bags of wool and marking the same ready for shipment. All the growers help each other, so we've had quite a picnic of sheep men in town today. All the work is not quite done so I'm spending the night in town instead of going to the ranch.

I spent the day in Colorado [City] yesterday, going down in the morning and returning last night. It's the first time I've been there to stop in several years, and while I used to be pretty well acquainted, I know scarcely any one there now. I went down there particularly to see if I could find any bricks for that chimney to our "shanty," but not one in the place for sale. I was quite at a loss for a while, because if I had been compelled to ship them from Fort Worth or Dallas, the chimney would eventually have cost more than the remainder of the house.

Thanks to man's inventive genius I think the problem has been solved. I had heard that such a thing was manufactured at the present time as an *iron* fireplace, simply needing an ordinary stove-pipe for a chimney, so I visited a hardware store, and with the assistance of the owner, looked through some of the advertising circulars sent him, soon finding the article for which we were in search.

The cut representing the arrangement looked very promising, and as the factory making them was no further off than Cincinnati, Ohio, I had one ordered. Whether it can be put into the wall so as to take place entirely of a fireplace or not, I do not know, but in other respects I think it will answer.

I thought of writing to you yesterday from Colorado [City] after I was through with what business I had, but met a young fellow with whom I used to go to school, and went up to his office and stayed nearly all the afternoon talking over old times and discussing our old school-mates with whose where-a-bouts either of us were acquainted.

It's curious how different some boys will turn out from what they promised when they *were* boys. I asked this fellow where a certain boy, Wills by name, was now. He said, "Wills is a banker in Dallas and worth likely fifty or sixty thousand dollars. You wouldn't have thought this of Wills, would you?" I told him, no, I shouldn't have thought it. Wills was about as dull in school as a boy could be, while many other of his class-mates, far ahead of him in intelligence, have not accomplished anything.

I guess this will reach you only a few days before *your* birth-day, and I wish I could follow the custom of other fellows who make their girls presents, not only on their birthdays but at various other times. If I were in some city where articles suitable for presents to young ladies were kept, I would be considerably puzzled to know what you'd like. As it is I'm not puzzled at all. I don't think there is anything in Marienfeld you'd *have*. I never thought of *this* advantage in living out here before.

A fellow can have a sweet-heart and love her ever so well and never be accused of thoughtlessness when he does not observe the above mentioned custom. It's useless for *me* to say under the circumstances that "I wish you many happy returns of the day." I trust each of our birth-days hereafter will find us so loving each other that all our actions will show, to ourselves at least, that this wish is the first in our minds.

I will be "awful" glad when the time comes for me to go down after you. I get rather lonesome sometimes, or I should say, this is my usual state. Every day now without you seems wasted. A *four* years engage-ment. I never thought before that Thad had any unusual powers of endurance, but I give him credit now for being something more than human.

I think the night of June 17th was the first time *I* knew you were going to let me "have my way." Not much over three months ago, but in looking back it seems the longest three months I ever lived.

If I write much more tonight I will begin to make "soft" remarks. When I write to you steady for a while without any interruption, everything *but* you passes out of my mind nearly altogether. I always picture you in imagination as I saw you last, standing on the steps after telling me good-bye, the most pleasing picture on which I ever looked, the most lovable little girl a man ever loved.

It's strange, but the four times I've told you good-bye, leaving out the one time I do not count when we parted out of temper, are more prominent in my memory than any other times when we were together. I suppose such times as these make a greater impression on a person's memory than any other. If people who loved each other were never to meet again, I guess their last farewell would be the longest remembered.

Good-night Sweetheart. While I love you every moment of my life, there are times when I feel as if you were dearer to me than others. Not this exactly, but I suppose I *can* love more at times. I need scarcely say tonight is one of these times. If this letter doesn't show it, then I have not been plain. This, however, is *bordering* on sentiment which you *sometimes* object to, so once more, good-night.

Affectionately Yours,
J.B.M.

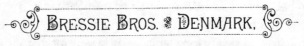

R. M. BRESSIE.   M. F. BRESSIE,   A. G. DENMARK.   W. Y. TENNYSON.   LANIE BRESSIE.

BRESSIE BROS. & DENMARK,

General Merchandise & Banking,

GRAIN AND RANCH SUPPLIES.

Fourth and Clinton Sts.,
and near Depot.

Big Springs, Texas. Oct 7th 1889

My Dear Little Girls,

I wonder how many more places there are yet from which you'll receive letters from me, and how many more kinds of letter heads I will use. My epistles to you would form quite a collection of the different styles of paper &c in use in Western Texas if they are preserved. I've been moving around as usual since I wrote last and while I stopped at maxedofeld yesterday and last night I did not get an expected letter from you. I suppose the mail of last night brot'

❧ 44 ❧

Bressie Bros. and Denmark
General Merchandise and Banking
Grain and Ranch Supplies
Fourth and Clinton Sts., and near Depot.
Big Springs, Texas, Oct. 7th, 1889

My Dear Little Girl,

I wonder how many more places there are yet from which you'll receive letters from me, and how many more kinds of letter heads I will use. My epistles to you would form quite a collection of the different styles of paper, etc., in use in Western Texas if they are preserved.

I've been moving around as usual since I wrote last, and while I stopped at Marienfeld yesterday and last night, I did not get an expected letter from you. I suppose the mail of last night brought me one, but I left too early this morning to get it.

Today I'm passing the time in one of the dullest places I ever visited. In my ramblings over this country, I always try to avoid Big Springs, that is, to stop for any length of time, but fate has willed it otherwise this time. I'm located here until nine o'clock tonight, or longer if the train happens to be late. I came in about six this morning, and as all the business I had to transact did not occupy more than half an hour, you perceive the day will not prove short. . . .

I went out to Midland Friday and was there until Sunday. Went to a spelling match Friday night at the schoolhouse, but as nature did not intend me to follow Mr. Webster's example, I did not accept the invitation to take part in the exercises, which was extended to the lookers on when the larger class was on the floor.

In the juvenile class a little five-year-old boy, said to be the "worst boy in town," spelled the last word given out after forty-nine of his class mates had retired from the contest, all larger than him, thereby winning for himself the honor of wearing the medal for the next month.

I noted this with secret satisfaction, thinking to myself that spellers, like poets, "were born, not made," and that a person is not altogether responsible, when they sometimes act independently of the dictionary and make spelling rules of their own.

Ella Mullinix informed me that the Midlanders, or rather the Midlandresses, the men of course do not speculate on such things, had settled it among themselves that she and I were to be married when that house was finished. She said she'd gotten tired of denying it, and now when questioned on the subject, admitted 'twas true. She thinks when her acquaintances find themselves mistaken, 'twill afford her ample satisfaction. As I am not personally acquainted with any of the Midlandresses myself, I suppose its not worth while to feel that I was being treated with injustice by not having credit given me of owning more discretion than to marry a girl not yet fifteen years old.

Another thing excusing them, the young ladies of M. old enough to take this step are such an undesirable lot, that a fellow *would* be to some extent justified, if he could not wait, in taking to himself a partner before she had been corrupted by evil communications. Fortunately, however, there are other places besides Midland, and other girls besides those there. The girl I have in my mind is as different from them as daylight is from darkness....

I hope I'll find a nice, long, letter from you tomorrow at Marienfeld, but I shan't promise to answer it at once. I know I'd repeat most of what I've written here, so will wait a day or two any way.

Well, good-bye. It's still sometime before night, but I won't inflict any more on you at present, but will try to get through the remaining hours as best I can. I know you'll hope after reading this, that I'll not spend the day in Big Springs again.

Yours, Aff.
J.B.M.

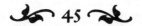

45

Marienfeld, Oct. 11/89

My Dear Mollie,

. . . I was out at Midland yesterday and the day before. The question, "When are you going to build your house?" is growing a trifle monotonous. Another, "What do you want with a house?" causes me to give very short answers. I guess the subject grows somewhat tiresome to you. If it did not worry me considerably, the idea of meeting with so many stumbling blocks during the last few months would appear ridiculous.

I've always intended things should be so arranged when I was married, that I could take life easy, but I don't know of a time during the last few years when every thing so conspired against ease as they do now. I'm not one that takes this world and the cares it brings very seriously, as you've probably heard me say before, but I do like to have my plans meet with a little more success than has been the case lately. Very likely, tho', I can look back in a year or two at this time of trouble and scarcely remember it.

The year, of course, will be one each of us will remember all our lives, but only as regards each other. *I* think its been one of more success to me than all those which have gone before. In remembering I have won for myself the regard of the dearest little girl in the world, I should not complain of ill-success in other undertakings. I know full well that, if necessary, I would sacrifice all other prospects tonight rather than lose your affection, for without it, all else would indeed be of little value. Then I'm inclined to think its not exactly necessary to have so much to contend against, even if I *have* got you to say nice things to, and have nice things said to me.

I'm inclined to do a good deal of useless fretting, knowing too, even if you hadn't told me not to, that is what *you'll* think. I know as well now as I will hereafter that you'll take things as you find them and never, even in your own mind, find fault. Still I can't help being bothered, altho' you order me not to be.

I never knew *your* mother well, so cannot compliment you by saying you are like *her*. But I remember my own, and while it's repeating, I think you have a great many traits of character very similar to her, and among them the one enabling you to be independent of your surroundings so far as regards your happiness.

Well, Sweetheart, I mustn't say it all tonight but leave a little until next time. I managed to get thro' the first four pages of this with pen and ink, but I had to make each letter twice before the pen would leave an impression. [I] concluded you would appreciate it none the less if I only wrote it once, even if I *did* use a pencil.

Good-night.

Yours Aff.
J.B.M.

Marienfeld Oct. 16/89

My Dear Mollie [and Judge McCormick],

I found your letter of the 9th awaiting me today on my return from Midland. If I had not become much better acquainted with your different moods lately, I *should* have thought [by] the general tone of it, such as *you* feared in reading it over, that you were trying to make me think you did not mean all you said in the one received just before. As very likely I'm in a similar mood myself tonight, I will not complain of your letter, so you must accept this in the same spirit, and if I do not come up to the standard required for a good letter, *imagine* what you would have liked for me to have said, as I did after reading yours.

I fear if this state of affairs lasts much longer, we each will be inclined to make short work of our letters to each other, and there-by convey wrong impressions. How the situation is to be bettered I know not. *I* cannot do without your letters at all, and I feel satisfied that you are glad to get mine, let them be what they may. . . .

I regret, as I've often said before, that I was so unfortunate as to give your father a wrong impression in regard to me. I find myself, for the first time in my recollection, the subject of anyone's continued displeasure. It's the first time also I've been in the present situation, so possibly my experience does not count for much. We will trust that in a few years, if I have succeeded in making you comfortable and happy, your father can say he has been "agreeably disappointed."

This section of the country is sending several of her representatives to the Dallas Fair, but I think I shall not be one of them this time.

A heavy rain yesterday and last night covered this part of the world with water, and has relieved me of considerable trouble for the present. My efforts in the direction of well boring are at a stand-still, and so far entirely unsuccessful. In a few days I intend to begin once more, on the old plan, that is, *digging* with pick and spade, and hope it will prove more effectual than has the improved method with machinery.

I have again borrowed the school-teacher's room and table for the preparation of this epistle, and again I think it's near his bed-time. So for the present, good-night.

Yours Aff.
J.B.M.

No. 2
Now, My Little Sweet-heart, I'll write *you* a little letter. When you ask me to write to you and your father, a partnership letter, for the next few weeks, you are asking next to an impossibility. In one way I do not care who sees my letters to you, nor who knows how much I love you, but when I try to confine myself to a style of composition which *you* would not object to having your father read, you see the result of my efforts in the part of this missive written with ink.

I tried twice to write to him and as many times failed, and while I'm perfectly willing to admit all his rights in our affairs, and also that children owe certain duties to their parents, I've had an idea of my own all along that *you* have a few rights, and that sometimes a parent owes duties to his children.

Mollie's father, Judge Andrew Phelps McCormick. Date of photograph is unknown, but it was taken by photographer G. Moses in New Orleans, where Judge McCormick presided over the United States Fifth Court of Appeals from 1892 to 1916.

I do not see how any stretch of the imagination could give your father the right to read my letters to you, nor do I think he would wish to. When he expressed his wish that he would rather be absent from home when we are married, so that he will not have the pleasure (?) of seeing me, his choice and mine in the matter are one. I do not think after this that he would be likely to have any desire to know what I should say to you.

If I could have arranged things so that we could have had a pleasant stopping place, I would have tried to have persuaded you to marry me before your father came home. You, of course, would have objected. But now where is the difference?

I do not like to write this way, and have so far kept from saying much about your father's course, knowing that I could very easily say *too* much. But when he "washes his hands," as it were, of the whole thing and says "you can do as you please" I think then he is asking more than his right when he wishes to read my letters to another after virtually declining to receive any more written to himself.

I wish he had seen fit to make things pleasant for you instead of the reverse, when he could so easily have done so. I cannot see his reason for wishing to make the taking of the most important step in your life unpleasant, when he could have made you much happier. But there's no use in saying any more about it.

I don't think, Little Girl, I can write you letters you'd appreciate if I have to try to write them to both of you. I *know* this. If I do, your father will not have his ideas of my ability as a letter writer improved any. I can't write you without telling you I love you, you know that, altho' in this letter I've not over-done it.

Once more, good-night,

Affectionately,

J-

Oct. 17. Your note received just before posting this. If I had time I would write you another letter instead of sending this one. As it is, I suppose I will have to wait. I cannot make out the name of the first street in the address you give me but will try to copy your writing, trusting the Dallas P.M. will understand.

❧ 47 ❧

Miss Mollie McCormick
c/o Mr. J.M.McCormick
Dallas, Texas
Oct.18, 1889

My Dear Little Girl,

If this proves as satisfactory to you as the writing of it does to me, then we are both happy. I think very seldom have I felt as much relieved as today, when I transferred all right, title and interest, in nearly all my four-footed beasts to another party. So I'm once more a free man, and shall place myself entirely at your disposal, for the present at least. I have some few things to attend to here which will occupy my time for three or four days.

From the present outlook, I think I will be in Dallas Tuesday or Wednesday. Quite a party will go from here Monday. I do not think I can go then, but possibly I may get off. Like you, I will not enlarge upon the subject which is now ever present with me. Remember me with thanks for their invitation to Manson and his wife.

Good-bye until I see you,
Yours Aff.
J.B.M.

NOTE: *In spite of his doubts, he does get to Dallas for a visit.*

48

Hotel Llano, A.F. Roland, Proprietor
Special Attention to Commercial Men
Rates, $2.00 per Day.
Midland, Texas, Oct. 30th, 1889

My Dear Little Girl,
    As no doubt you will be expecting a letter by the first mail which
I could possibly use, I will try not to disappoint you, altho' I shall confine myself to a few words. I think it a fortunate thing for you in one
respect that our days of correspondence are numbered or very nearly so.
I'm afraid my reputation as a letter writer, if I have one, would likely suffer if I were destined to keep up my end of the line much longer. You,
if compelled to read every few days one of my worn out epistles would
find it quite a strain on your affections to *love* me much longer.
    With the memory of the last moments we spent together fresh in
my mind, it seems such a falling off to confine oneself to a letter. Anything written seems so unsatisfactory in comparison.
    The trip up yesterday and the larger part of last night as usual was
tiresome, the train reaching here about one o'clock, nearly two hours
late, not helping matters any. I frequently compared the surroundings
yesterday, with what they will likely be when next I come from Dallas
here. In one way particularly was the contrast very striking.
    Yesterday morning at the hotel, I heard a fellow say he was coming
out to Midland. Before I noticed he had been drinking, I asked him if
he lived in this section, never having seen him before. He said yes, and
when informed that such was the case with me, he asked me if I wouldn't
take charge of him, and see him safely through. Said he had been on a
"spree" for several days, and needed a protector. I believe it's the only
time I ever felt my sympathy overcoming my disgust for a man in his
condition, so I told him I would take him home.
    He was far above the ordinary drunkard, or I guess I should have
declined to help him. He gave me his ticket, what money he had, and
a gold watch chain, having already been robbed of his watch, and told

me to keep them until he was sober. He gave me no trouble whatever, sleeping nearly the whole way here. I turned him over in good shape to the hotel man, who knew who he was.

Our house has made rapid progress since I left, and the contractor says the carpenter work will be done by Saturday night. The "finishing up" will likely take another week after that or longer, but I think we can safely say 'twill be habitable by Saturday week. I think the furniture will be here in a few days, certainly by that time.

So now, Sweetheart, after keeping you in uncertainty for so long, I will leave the rest in your hands, and be waiting to come for you any time after our home is ready.

If this letter sounds cool, I do not mean it so, but you know this.

Yours Affectionately,
J.B.M.

Midland, Nov. 8, 1889

My Dear Mollie,

For the same reason that you did not write sooner, I have not written a second time, but I'd fully made up my mind to write you again today whether I heard from you or not. Strange to say your long silence has not worried me near so much this time as it has done heretofore. I could guess pretty well that you were feeling the same as I felt, not up to a long letter and feared I would complain at a short one. Nor do I feel the least bit disappointed that you did not send me a longer letter. I think I know you somewhat better now than I "used to," and am more able to sympathize with your "off and on" spells. I guess in letter writing it should be as in conversation, we ought to understand each other well enough to not feel *forced* to talk.

Our new house is progressing somewhat slowly, it seems to me. I guess it's because I'm in such a hurry. Things will be in readiness as soon as we are. That stove was so long coming I began to think it was lost, but it came in a few days ago. The furniture is here, but I haven't taken it from the depot yet.

I notice cards out this morning for a "grand hop" at the courthouse tonight. Guess I'll have to go and act as "wall flower." It may be my last appearance. You say *you'll* not go without you dance, and I'll hardly go without you, *soon* anyway.

I hope your father may think better of our arrangements, before we are married, but I hardly think he will. It's hard on you, but I think now 'twould be much harder to try to comply with his wishes. In fact, it would be utterly impossible to say we would abide by his decision, and mean what we said.

As we are likely to have ample opportunities for the exchange of ideas during the coming years, I will, for this time, call this enough.

Affectionately,

J.B.M.

NOTE: *J.B.M. does not feel the need to write at length, as they plan to marry the following week, giving them "ample opportunities" for conversation. When next he is in Midland, however, Mollie is not with him.*

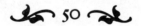

Midland, Nov. 17, '89

My Dear Little Girl,

You are already well aware of the fact that my assurances of not writing to you are not to be relied upon, but when I left you last, I did really think I had said all I could well say. Many thoughts, however, have presented themselves since then, and as you said positively you'd not write first even if I had nothing to say for myself, I'm already most anxious to hear from you.

As our feelings about each other are getting to be somewhat equal,

I need not try to describe to you my state of mind during the time since I told you good-bye. The day I came from Dallas was not particularly the happiest I ever passed. If I'd done a little more thinking or could have imagined more clearly what the delay in our plans would cost us, I think I can say, I doubt whether I could have come away as easily as I did.

Several times I thought seriously of retracing my steps, feeling almost certain that you were thinking, "Well, if he were back here now he would not go off alone." Was I right, Sweetheart? I'm glad, tho', that my generosity prevailed over selfishness, and that I have not made your position any harder by trying to urge you to act differently.

The house, one room of which I've been occupying since my return, feels rather lonesome. I miss you as much as if you had been here and were gone.

Ella M- was rather disappointed and I've had to defend you so much against her attacks, that I've almost persuaded myself that I alone am responsible. She said this morning she'd bet if she were old enough and wanted to marry a fellow, no one would stop *her*. I asked her if the fellow himself wanted it put off, what she'd do, telling her that I was the sole cause of your not coming back with me.

When I went down town yesterday morning, the question was repeatedly asked, if congratulations were in order. One fellow says, "John, this ain't right. You are fooling the people too much." I could have told him the people were no worse off than me, but did not.

The next time I leave for the same purpose, I think I'll have this insertion placed in the paper: "J.B. McGill has gone to Marienfeld for a few days." I don't think it possible for them to say he has gone there for a wife. This part of the business, however, does not bother me in the slightest. I find it rather amusing than otherwise.

Now, Sweetheart, there is one feature of the case which I entirely overlooked, or at least did not think of it the night we said good-bye. Since then in going over things in my own mind I have imagined this, and am almost certain that such will be the case, altho' I trust I'm wrong. I think your father has the intention, if he can, of stopping it. Everything points this way, his endeavors to bind us by a promise, etc.

You remember I told you long ago, I couldn't help feeling somehow that something would happen to separate us. This feeling, of course, does not make things any easier. I know I have your promise to marry me in March, and it does not seem that I place much faith in your promise to have any fears of this kind, but I can't help it.

I know that your father has a great influence over you if he tries to exert it. I've said before that the man who had a promise from you could rest as secure as he could in a promise from the Bible that it would be kept. My presentiments that something would happen had almost disappeared with what we thought was the approach of our wedding. This delay has made them stronger than ever.

Be true to me, Little Girl, as I will to you, adverse influence not-withstanding. When the time comes, marry me, not because you have promised, but because you love me.

If things grow unpleasant for you from any cause, or you find the consciousness of trying to please your father does not make you as happy as you think you'd be in a home of your own, remember that home is waiting for you. In it you will always be loved as you will no-where else.

Please write me soon. Aside from the fact that I'm always impatient for one of your letters, I'll admit at the present time I have some curiosity as to the progress of events with you.

Affectionately,
J.B.M.

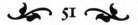

Midland, Nov. 23, 1889

My Dear Little Girl,

I know you'll be expecting a letter and will feel disappointed if it does not come, but I fear you'll be more disappointed in this than you would in none at all. I'm not up to the mark of writing just yet. I've been trying to frame a letter in my mind all day, but have not succeeded. I don't think I fully realized the hardness of the task which we have to accomplish before today.

I had been hoping all the week past, that after a few days reflection, you would tell me to come back again. I was sorely disappointed when I learned you were going home [to Graham] again.

I know your position will be harder than mine, in many ways, and I do not want to make it any harder by complaining. You have one consolation which I have not. You are obeying the unreasonable demands of an unreasonable father. While I do not want you to do anything which you think might cause you regret hereafter, I think you are making a mistake. I know full well that the next three months for you will be most unhappy.

I think we belonged to each other as much on Thursday night, as we would have so belonged on Friday morning after the wedding. I do not think *any* one ought to have tried to separate us, or at least have succeeded in their efforts.

I cannot place myself, as I said before, in your position, so do not know how much your idea of obedience would allow you to be imposed upon. I've often wondered if it would not have been better, and would still be better, to try to persuade you to take things in your hands. I know 'twould be useless to try anything of this kind unless I acted the selfish part, and worked on your sympathies through your affection for me, something I shall not do, with selfish intent at least.

Don't imagine from this, Sweetheart, that I'm anything like patient. I've been growing "madder" every day since I left Dallas. If my anger increases in proportion until March, my affection for your father will be something beautiful to behold. I guess we had a lucky escape when we did not promise him to abide by his decision in the matter. We'd very likely been worse off now than we are, and we are not particularly "well fixed" at present.

I was guilty of attending another dance last night, but I must confess my dancing was more from a sense of duty than anything else. I don't think I can keep to my promise of going to everything this winter. I think when I get this house fixed to my notion I'll go to the country and spend most of the time.

I discharged all the workmen when I came home, and have been busy since finishing up. I'm getting to be quite a painter, oil colors altogether. I guess I'll take up your carpet and fold it carefully away until spring. 'Twill need cleaning by March anyway, and I don't feel at home on a carpet alone.

In waiting for your letters from this [time] on, I'll be just as I was last winter, thinking certainly the next one will be the one for which I'm waiting.

You must not expect me to write the same as I used to, Little Girl. I can't do it. I do not expect many fellows are ever disappointed as badly as I was last week, and I can't drop back to the old way of writing letters after that. I know you can't either, so we'll write the best we can, and agree not to find fault with each other.

I think you remarked once that you liked to use a pencil where you did not care for appearances, so next time you do not have pen and ink follow my example, and rest perfectly easy that I will be as glad to get one from you, as you will to get this. I'm not a bit conceited, am I?

Don't wish you could write differently from what you can. I know you love me just as well as if you had told me so, and this knowledge goes along way towards helping me through with the present hard and needless arrangement.

Good-night, Sweetheart-I expect I might say, Little Wife, without being very far off. We came awful near it, didn't we?

Affectionately Yours,
J.B.M.

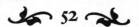

52

Midland, Dec. 2, 1889

My Dear Little Girl,
I intended not to write until I had an answer from my last letter, but several days have gone by since I was due and as I did not wish to keep

the enclosed letters waiting any longer I will forward them and inflict a few lines on you extra. I send a copy of my reply to Janie's, so if you care to answer it too, you can see what I wrote. I guess the one unopened [addressed to Mrs. J.B. McGill] is intended for you, and the necessity of its being forwarded does not make the situation any more cheerful.

I wonder if the past two weeks have been as hard on you as on me. I hope not, because between a desire to please your father and your inclination to do otherwise, you have not been exceedingly happy.

I can't write, Sweetheart, without making you feel worse, there's no use in trying. I thought possibly I could grow a little more patient after a while, but I think about you from morning until late at night, and find myself inclined to get more *im*patient instead.

I guess you grew tired sometimes of my complaining letters several months ago, and think while reading some of these if another lot has to be endured *your* patience will be severely tried, but I know if I did not write at all, you'd not appreciate it. While I've tried my utmost to submit calmly to the order of things, I find it impossible to write you without a gentle reminder that so far I've failed.

I invested in a photograph frame the other day, and now that picture of you occupies a prominent place on the mantel in this room. It might be considered all imagination by many that a mere picture is any company, but there's no other article on these premises which has a greater value to me than that picture. In case of fire, I'm perfectly certain that your photograph would be the first thing considered. I guess you little thought when having them taken that one of the lot would ever be thought as much of as this one.

I had a young fellow from Marienfeld to stay all night with me last week, and we were discussing affection of different kinds. He's been married nearly a year, and remarked if there was any difference in the regard between him and his wife, he thought his wife loved him the most. I told him I didn't know how 'twould be when we were married, but at the present time, if you loved me as I did you, this mansion would have a house-keeper. I don't mean you to understand that I have any doubt of your affection, because I have none, and I believe *you* think you have quite as much regard for me as I have for you, but when I *know* there's not a man, woman, or child on the face of this frost-bitten earth for whose wishes I'd postpone our happiness one day, then I'm forced to think your affection is just 3 ½ months behind mine. I believe I *have* loved you this much longer anyway, haven't I, Sweetheart?

I have been thinking a good deal lately that what your father said to you on your return from school would be applicable in this case. That as 'twould not be long before you and Mrs. McCormick would have to decide on who was "boss," you'd just as well begin when you went home.

I know from experience that you are hard to convince that my prophecies are right, but I will venture one more, that Judge McCormick will be in Graham between now and March, will not let you know he is coming, and will not stay long enough for you to send for me. What plan of action he will pursue in M'ch has not yet been revealed to me, nor does it make much difference. I know you will give yourself to me then, but, Little Girl, I do hate to wait.

I went to church this morning for the first time in Midland, and heard quite a good sermon from the new Methodist minister. I've given up ball going, found the strain to be gay and festive once a week too much.

I wish you'd tell me when you answer this, whether you'd appreciate silence on my part more than you would a letter of this kind or some possibly a little more so. Unless there's something especial needing a reply in the one I *ought* to get tomorrow, I guess I'll bear my sufferings in silence until you answer this one.

Yours Aff.
J.B.M.

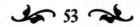

53

Midland, Dec. 5, 1889

My Dear Little Girl,
    Such letters as the one I enclose to you coupled with the fact that I've not had a line from you for nearly two weeks does not keep me in a good humor.
    If you can answer this one [from Aunt Kate], its more than I can do. I answered the one from Janie, so I think you might write to Aunt Kate. I think also you might write to me once a week at any rate, altho' don't think I want to *limit* you. I expect you find it rather hard to write. So do I, but you know I want to hear from you occasionally. Whether your letters suit you or not, I will understand and appreciate them.
    I sometimes get the impression that you have learned how much you are to me. Then when you make me wait so long for a letter, I feel certain you do not, and do not always realize myself what the loss of you would mean to me, but when I am forced to imagine such a thing by a longer silence than usual on your part, it does not seem possible that life *could* look so hopeless.
    Good-night, Sweetheart. If I were to make a generous wish, I'd hope you are happy without me, but [I] don't hope anything of the kind.

Yours Affectionately,
J.B.M.

[Enclosure postmarked Austin, Dec. 3, 1889]
Mr. John B. McGill, Midland, Midland Co., Texas

Dear John and Mollie,
    This is the first letter of congratulation I ever attempted to write, I believe, so if it does not come up to your ideas of the fitness of things, I will have to implore you, as you, John, did in your youthful days of your audiences, not to "view it with a critic's eye, but pass its imperfections by." [A footnote says, "A remark I never made -J-"]

I can at any rate very sincerely say I wish you much happiness. I am not going to inflict advice upon you at this time to any great extent, but I will, in the language of another, commend to your consideration the two great Bears, BugBear and Forbear. I believe the more their acquaintance is cultivated the better. That may be stated as a truth in any, and every, relation of life, but it is especially true in the marriage relation.

Your relatives in Austin are tolerably well, I believe, tho' I cannot speak with certainty of your Father and sisters, John, as I have not heard very directly. I have sold my old Horse and Carriage and have no way to get around now except to walk and as friends take me. I hope you will write to them tho' and find out for yourself.

I suppose you knew the Church was being finished. It is torn to pieces and we are now worshipping with the Southern Methodists. It is a pleasant Church and it is pleasant to be with them for they are very cordial in their Hospitality, but we feel sometimes as if we were crowding them. However, they say not, and seem really glad to have us.

The Cumberland Presbyterians have it in contemplation to build a Church, I believe, also. They have an entertainment for the purpose of raising money this week. I think it is called a Kermiss. I suppose it will be quite unique and very interesting to lovers of Novelties. The Ladies of our Church give one the following week. I think their entertainment will be called an International Teaparty. Booths will be arranged representing the different Nationalities, appropriate music will be Selected and *executed*!! There will be a Supper and Lunches for two days. There is much work connected with it but it devolves mostly upon the Young Ladies, Married and Single.

We are having beautiful weather now. I hope for the Sake of those interested in the entertainments it will continue some time.

Jennie sends love to both of you. Hoping and praying for God's best gifts for you.

I am yours affectionately,
C.E. Bell

Midland, Dec. 8, 1889

My Dear Little Girl,

I owe you two letters I believe, one rec'd yesterday and one this morning. I wish you'd instruct your mail carrier or your P.M. to send letters addressed to me the first opportunity. The one dated Dec. 3 reached me yesterday, the one dated Dec. 1st reached me today being postmarked Dec 5th.

The first one rec'd but the last written was very short and should have been sweet, but your uneasiness as to what the Midland P.M. would think of a letter addressed to Mrs. McGill seems to have prevented any tender remarks. From the general tone of it I should judge the awkwardness of the situation, as regards what people say, was worrying you more than the knowledge that I was wearing myself out in *im*patient waiting, and I'm afraid justifying your assertion that I was a "Crank," the only pet name you ever gave me. I fear, too, that what I said in my note enclosing Aunt Kate's letter will lead you to think that I bother myself about what people think.

Now on this point, Sweetheart, you can rest easy. I have my box at the Post Office and the P.M. or his sister who stays there is paid to distribute the mail. It's none of their business if I have to forward your letters to Graham. As they do not know you under your own name nor the one to which you say you lay no claim, I do not think you need worry yourself over the affair. *I* do not any more than it reminds me of, not "what might have been," but what ought to have been, that is, if a reminder were necessary.

There is another young fellow here in the same fix I am, so far as I can guess. He went down as far as Ft. Worth on the same train with myself the other day, but I did not know until I returned that he went to get married. *He* had been having his house put in order for some time past. A day or two ago he returned alone, and rented out his house. I'm not very well acquainted with him so we've not exchanged confidences.

'Twas not the same trouble with him tho', I know, for his girl has been living with her brother-in-law for the last few years and if she had a father I don't know where he is.

The only bother I've had regarding outsiders are applications to rent *this* house. I generally tell them "no," it's not for rent, and the chances are they want to know why. To make matters worse, I told several during its construction that I was building it *to* rent. I suppose I could tell them 'twas not mine, but this would necessitate a still longer explanation.

I had one applicant thru' Mrs. Mullinix that I was disposed to accommodate. A new music teacher wanted one room in which to place her piano. I sent her word she could have it rent free if she'd furnish her own stove. I've not met her myself but think very likely she may persuade me to even furnish the stove, *herself.* If this comes to pass, you can imagine me consoling myself with the music teacher, while you and the Methodist parson are enjoying your flirtation. Possibly under these circumstances I may become as philosophical as you are.

But enough of other people, now for ourselves. The more extensive my acquaintance becomes with you, the less I flatter myself that I understand the female character. I feel almost certain that you'd have thought more of me today, if I'd used my powers of persuasion while in Dallas the last night to get you to carry out our original plan. I'm afraid you are a little inclined to blame me in your mind for the existing state of affairs, and think I submitted too easily.

I know I had your assurance on that night that you'd not love me any less because I gave up to you, but notwithstanding, I've regretted very frequently that I left you as I did. I guess tho' now we are on even ground. I resolved long ago to marry you if I *could*. As you seem to have made the same resolution as regards me, I suppose next time we'll have better luck. Provided your ideas of a *providential* interference are not too general, and you do not look upon human agency as a decree of providence.

I've said enough disagreeable things for one letter, so I'll draw on my imagination (!) a little and say something pleasant as a farewell.

Every new complication which arises in our career makes it clearer to me that you are the most perfect little woman or the dearest little girl, which ever you like better, that I ever knew. I know perfectly well that you are as much worried over things as they are as I am, still no word of complaint have I read. I've learned long since, or thought I had, to be patient myself, but you will hardly believe this now. If, after we do join hands, our hearts I guess are already so, you are as patient and uncomplaining under difficulties as you have been since I have known you, then instead of writing you that you are the Dearest Little Girl, I can tell you face to face so you'll know I believe it, that you are the Dearest Little Wife.

Affectionately Yours,
J.B.M.

❧ IV ❧

Affectionately Yours

Midland, Dec. 12, 1889

My Dear Little Girl,

If I hadn't written you a comparatively decent letter Sunday, the same time you wrote to me, and very likely received by you last night, I would certainly feel very much conscience stricken after reading the one I got today. I believe if I could count on getting such a letter from you every morning, I might possibly endure the next three months with something like creditable fortitude. I'm well aware of the fact that most of my letters to you since I saw you last have not been such as would keep your spirits up, and when this last one came I realized more fully than ever how hard I had been on you, and how nice you could treat a fellow even when he didn't deserve it.

I believe four weeks of our waiting expires tonight, and next Sunday I think will be one year since you and Thad met me down at the depot in Austin. Taking it all together I guess I've seen some of the happiest moments and some of the gloomiest during the last twelve months thru' which I've ever passed.

I think I've read somewhere that to have your mind fixed on one subject without the power to change is in itself insanity. I don't know how long this state of things has to continue before the thinker becomes a full grown lunatic, but if one year's thinking is enough, then I'm nearly ready for the asylum. I've often thought during this time that when people *do* go crazy, that instead of being objects of pity to observers they were rather to be envied. I know I frequently wished during some of my blue spells that if the power to *forget* were not given me, then that the ability to *feel* would be taken away.

But these desires to the contrary, notwithstanding, I still have the faculty of thinking about and loving you more every day, and feel no particular weakening of the intellect either. *I* might be the last one to discover this latter fact, however.

I've not been anticipating any extra pleasures for Christmas, but this is nothing new for me. Since the Christmas of '78, the last one I spent in Austin, the occasion has not been different from the days before and after. Last year in Lampasas I was just beginning a new era in my history, being in love, and trying to figure how much or how little your first letter meant, and looking forward to seeing you soon. Since then every thought or every idea of "having a good time" has been connected directly with you, and will be thro' all the coming years. If the day ever comes when I can't anticipate enjoyment with you, then all speculations as to enjoyment at all will be things of the past. . . .

I'm no more superstitious than you are, but I have a continual dread hanging over me nearly all the time that you and I will never be any nearer married than we have been. This makes the delay much harder than it would be ordinarily. I try to shake off the feeling but something comes up again to make me think of and worry over it. Once or twice in your late letters you have emphasized providentiality. I've had a cold myself and so has nearly every one I've heard from in this section, but I've never been the least uneasy as to anything happening on *my* part either physically or from any other cause to prevent our happiness. I don't think I'll refer to this feeling any more tho'. I don't want you to take up the same notion. It's not a very pleasant sensation.

I haven't been out of Midland since I came from Dallas. I guess I've occupied the same sleeping place longer this "spell" than for some time before. I've kept busy during the day and the time when I can work has passed off more quickly than I would have supposed, but the long evenings get "kinder" lonesome. I can't sleep near all night and do not like to go to bed before eleven o'clock. I sometimes think of inflicting a letter on you oftener than I do, but fear 'twould be repeating too much what I've said before.

I suppose I *might* get acquainted with some of the fair "Midland-esses" and call on them now and then, if I'd not acquired the unfortunate habit lately of drawing contrasts between you and other women decidedly unfavorable to the latter. This may be flattering to you, but it always makes me wish I was somewhere else. At least I think it would. I haven't made many calls lately.

I pass away an hour or two nearly every night helping the two older Mullinix girls with their next day's lessons, but they have a way of holding their books themselves, Geographies, for instance, and asking me where certain places are-which is more convenient for them than looking on the map.

I'm glad on your account that we have received the congratulatory letters which we have from Austin. In one way I know it makes no more difference to you than to me what they thought of it, but I should prefer they would look on it with kindly eyes.

I think we are more likely to have less to contend with in our married life living out here than we would among our kindred. I trust both of us will always be welcome guests at any of the homes of our relations. If we are not then we won't have to call for the sake of appearances. While it may be somewhat selfish, we need not worry ourselves over the hardships other members of the family have to undergo, and our own difficulties will be overcome by ourselves without the sympathy or assistance of our brothers, sisters, uncles, or aunts.

Well, good-night, Sweetheart. The train has just passed, and this is my usual time for retiring. I don't think I mentioned the fact before that the morning which was to have been our wedding day this train did not leave Dallas until *ten* o'clock. We'd have had a nice time at the depot, wouldn't we?

Aff. Yours,
J.B.M.

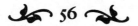 56

Midland, Dec. 15, 1889

My Dear Little Girl,

Thanks to Mr. Parker for sending your last letter the quickest route. I was very agreeably surprised when I went to the Post Office this morning. Differing from the short one I rec'd some days ago, *this* one was very satisfactory. I could say 'twas a nearer approach to "sweet" than any I have had before, but I know you'd think I was laughing at you, when I would be very far from it.

I never have in my own mind, altho' I may have said things to cause you to think it, doubted your love for me. Your reticence on the subject has never given me a moment's anxiety. Still, when you do unbend a little as you have in this last letter and *tell* me you *do* think a good deal of me, I like to read it. I know your "good deal" means more than hundreds of other women would mean in covering a dozen pages with affectionate passages.

This is about the only thing about which I have no doubts about being deserving, our mutual affection, or rather our love for each other. I rest very secure in the belief that no matter what points of superiority you now have or may hereafter develop over me, you will never love me any more than I do you. I have sometimes feared, knowing how seldom you ever said anything about loving me in your letters, that mine to you might prove tiresome, but if you *still* like to have me tell you the truth, the very truth, and nothing but the truth, in this regard, I guess my fears are groundless.

This is one draw-back about letter writing as compared to personal interviews. You and I could be together quite a while without the use of *spoken* language, and make known to each other by *signs* or other means of communication, the opinion we entertained of each other, far more satisfactorily than saying it. While in letter writing, if we were to leave a few blank lines like these-

-to be filled in by the imagination, 'twould be merely a waste of paper.

The foregoing brings to mind the poetical effusion I read to you and Thad just a year ago, lacking a day or two, which caused you and him such a desire to laugh. I've never yet learned the "funny" part of it, but I guess we can both appreciate love-making in any way now, better than we could then.

A year ago tomorrow, we went to church together, and then spent the afternoon at the Bakers'. I guess the date of my falling in love is not so hard to settle upon as a great many fellows'. I think it began on that memorable Sunday, grew, and almost matured by Tuesday night. All my questions to you on the subject have never given me any light as to when you began to love me. Notwithstanding the long weary months you kept me in suspense, I'm inclined to think your regard for me was more than you thought when we told each other good-bye Tuesday night.

I didn't go to church this morning, but 'twill save repetition to remark when I *do* go. I *did* intend to go today, however, but heard there would be no preaching, and did not learn otherwise until too late. I *may* go tonight. There's a new Methodist church being built here, so if you are desirous of changing your membership, why not wait until you change your residence and name? I guess you are not very particular about changing (churches I mean).

Now I've written this much without "fussing" and for fear my resolution *not* to fuss this time will not last much longer, I'd better cease. Especially as I may have to put still another strain on it when I answer the letter I shall expect tomorrow.

The music teacher, I guess, has found another room. I have heard nothing from her lately, so even this consolation is denied me in my time of need. I'm not in a writing mood tonight and as you are already in my debt two letters, I will wait as I promised in my last until you "settle up."

Aff. Yours,
J.B.M.

NOTE: *Unexpectedly, he goes to Graham for a Christmas week visit.*

Thomson House (formerly Sikes House.)
J.R. Thomson, Proprietor
Feather beds in Winter and South Rooms in Summer
Good Bath and Sample Rooms

Weatherford, Texas, Jan. 1st, 1890

My Dear Little Girl,

To tell you the honest truth, this is written more to keep you from being disappointed than anything else, but I expect the mere fact of my telling you this, will make it less appreciated than it otherwise would be. I slept, I think, about three hours last night, and do not feel much in a letter writing mood at the present time.

I am "sorter" struggling between a resolution and an inclination, a resolution to not write you any more "blue" epistles, and an inclination to write like I feel. Strange to say I haven't felt very much depressed until tonight.

Miss Ada proved to be a very agreeable traveling companion, and won my liking from the very start by saying Cousin Mollie was the nicest one of you four girls. As she made the remark several times and gave her reasons for so thinking, I know she really thinks so, and did not make the assertion to please me. She got very tired before we reached here, and I think rather nervous after dark. She did not seem to consider that she was as safe as if her father or brother were with her.

After telling her good-bye at her friend's house, it seemed as if the last link between the "winding up" of the old year and the beginning of the new had been broken and a reaction began with me resulting in the struggle mentioned above.

I wish I was at Midland tonight without the prospect of the trip tomorrow. I believe I hate it more than the stage ride.

As no doubt our feelings at the present moment are of a sameness, I will resist the *inclination*, for this once at least, and not harrow *your* feelings more than they are already harrowed. I will just refer you to yourself and say I'm suffering with a similar complaint.

I'm afraid to begin on the *affectionate* style because I fear 'twill drift from this to the less attractive one of despondency, so again I will refer you to yourself and say as you love me so do I feel towards you. Never until I'd been with you this time have I felt that I would be comparatively safe in saying this. Even now I can hardly realize that my little girl *does* love me so much.

If I meet Dr. & T. Stiles on the train tomorrow, possibly I can pass part of the time away easily in hearing the Austin news. . . .

Ever Aff yours,
J.B.M.

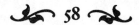

Midland, Jan. 3, 1890

My Dear Little Girl,

I know no other fellow ever had a sweetheart who could send him a handsome Xmas present and be with him a whole week before he rec'd it and not tell him *something* about it, but leave him to be very pleasantly surprised when he otherwise might have lost *part* of the appreciation by being forewarned. *You* have very likely missed being thanked in a more satisfactory manner than by letter, but I will endeavor to make it up in the years to come.

I am like you in not being very demonstrative except on rare occasions. So a mere "thank you very much," means more with me than a more effusive show of appreciation would mean with many. . . .

You will learn from this that instead of regretting having paid you a visit, as I thought possibly I might, I'm very, very glad I went to see you. I've been repenting more than you would think, tho', of saying things that hurt you, two or three times. If its any consolation to you, however, it hurt me more immediately after they were said than it hurt you, and I guess longer.

I regret, too, the discussion we had about the cards.* As you very likely have known all the time that I would do as you liked, its hardly worth while to say that if it's ultimately decided that we must have them, I will send you a list of the Midland citizens. When I begin, I will hardly know where to leave off. *Intimate* friends are few and far between. Ordinary or business acquaintances several.

Another thing in connection with this. Whenever you and I are brought into an argument, please don't try to end it by giving in to me as you did in this case, and have once or twice before. I know every tone of your voice almost as well as I do the features of your face, and when you say, "Very well, if you wish it," it worries me much longer than you would think. The time may come, I trust it never will, when you will give way to me and feel that I'm having my own way over yours, but not yet, Little Girl, not yet. I would rather argue until we are both tired, than hear you say "very well" the way you can say it.

Dr. Stiles *was* on the train yesterday, and I found him much more inquisitive regarding my movements than when he was *going* to Austin. I told him the folks down there could give him more information than I could myself, so 'twas no use in answering his questions. I learned very little from him in regard to family items of interest.

We have another young gentleman cousin, I believe by the name of Andrews. Cousin Lucy and mother-in-law are keeping the same house. You remember asking me who was living with her. He seemed to be very much concerned that Mary should have an engagement liable to be continued so long. Whether he had any personal interest in the matter I can't say.

Charlie Andrews has actually found a girl to whom he could engage himself, and was then idiot enough to break it off himself. R. Spence was heard to remark that if Charlie could become engaged, he didn't see why he couldn't.

The Dr. said he wished he'd stayed in Abilene for Xmas so I inferred Austin was dull.

Dull times are complained of here, so I'm of the opinion that you and I are fortunate in having a good time. If the New Year makes the future more hope-ful to you, and the next 2 ½ months seem not *very* long, then we can congratulate ourselves not only on a "Merry Christmas" but a "Happy New Year."

I realize that in one sense this letter is not very complimentary to you, my being in comparatively good spirits, but I've written so many that seemed as if I were sure enough "in the depths," it will, I know, make you much happier to have one when I'm out of them.

I've several times in different ways remarked on my ability to be happy under adverse circumstances. Since I've seen you last I will subside, with the conviction forced upon me that you are much my superior in this regard. Our lives together *ought* to be, with our dispositions united, very happy. I think they will be. I will be impatient to get your first letter, to see what effect the visit had upon you. 'Twould be curious now, wouldn't it, if *I* had to turn comforter.

Ever Aff. Yours,
J.B.M.

* He refers to engraved cards announcing the marriage.

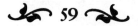

59

Midland, Jan. 11, 1890

My Dear Little Girl,
I found your letter awaiting me as I anticipated when I came in this afternoon. It was about two o'clock when I came in and I proceeded over to the Mullinix's to hunt some dinner. Mrs. M. brought me your letter and seemed surprised that I did not read it before eating, but I told her when a fellow had lost his appetite as often as I have by reading a letter just before a meal, he'd learned to eat first. . . .

I came back from where I've been "well digging" by way of Marienfeld and stayed there last night, so did not get here quite as soon as I expected. I guess this business of digging wells has grown monotonous to you. So you can realize what it must be to me when I've been at it nearly six months, and couldn't now get a drink of water on the land unless I carried it with me from somewhere else.

If it were not a matter of almost absolute necessity, I would give it up, but if there's any possibility to succeed it has to be done. Where there are plenty of excellent wells on all sides and some within two miles of where I've been at work, it does seem strange I've had such luck. I'm going back again tomorrow and "try, try again." Since I managed to persuade you that you could be an affectionate woman, I've more than ever felt like I could accomplish what I undertook.

I brought my horses up from Marienfeld today, and guess now I will try to keep them in the same county, at least, that the buggy is. They haven't seen it since the first part of November. I drove out here then, but the horses seemed to prefer their old range, and I've had very little use for them since, so let them stay. I expect I'll be away until the latter part of next week, and if it's any consolation to you to know that it's as hard for me to do without your letters as it is for you not to get mine, then you can be consoled.

I don't know what's coming over me in the last few nights in the way of dreams. I've dreamed about you several times lately. One rather peculiar. It seems that another girl turned up for whom I imagined I had a greater regard than for you. I did what you've always said you wanted me to do in such a case, engaged myself to the other girl.

The arrangements were all made, but as the time for the wedding approached I began to make comparisons decidedly unfavorable to your successor. When the day was drawing very near, I was in a state more deplorable than any I can remember being in during my waking hours. At this stage of the dream I awoke, and I think the relief I felt at its not being real would make you feel very easy over the prospect of never having a rival in earnest. I know if any other girl *should* turn up, the memory of what I felt in my dream would compel me to give her a wide berth. As I've not made any acquaintances in the young lady line lately, there was no visible cause for my imagination taking such a turn during sleep. As you are somewhat familiar with my letters now, its not worth while to say I do not often take up so much space in recounting dreams.

Do you know, Little Girl, that unless you've learned differently recently, you are laboring under a wrong impression as to the day on which falls the 14th of March. I don't think I ever before went this far into the New Year without seeing several new almanacs, but last night was the first I noticed for 1890, and Friday is certainly the day on which we are at present calculating.

I, like you, have no superstition in regard to Friday, but as there are six more days we might have one of them.[1] Don't, however, on my account let it make any new disturbance between you and your father. It's possible tho' he may have overlooked this fact himself, and would prefer Thursday.

Midland is rather on the sick-list right now with the measles, and that new complaint "La Grippe."[2] At least they think the number of colds indicate this. I have a very moderate headache tonight myself, and a very slight sore throat, but do not imagine I'm contracting any serious indisposition.

The Baptist revivalist is going to continue his meetings during next week so I suppose he's having some encouragement. I guess this is the best town in the West, religiously speaking.

Don't you think, judging from my last letter and the part of this you've read, I'm making vast strides towards leaving out any hint even of affection? I just read this over, and have actually completed ten pages without saying anything "soft." I never made any resolution of this kind either. I never used to think it could be done, but the way the thing is now, it seems, not exactly useless, but as if you'd think while you read it, "Well, I know all this, and he's just writing it to please me." I've begun to realize lately tho' the full sense of the term "better half" as applied to a man's wife.

It seems that loving you was a thing that went without saying and that you had become such a necessity as to really be a part and very essential part of my make-up. If I were to lose you in any way 'twould seem, leaving out the mental and moral sense of loss, as if I *had* lost half of myself physically.

If you feel as I do, and I know you do to a great extent, that if we could for a moment forget that we loved each other, still to live our lives apart, we'd feel as if something had gone from them. To make up your mind now that we were *not* to be married, you would consider a greater change than you thought a year ago would be to *get* married. I don't expect you to admit this, because you think "admissions are dangerous" but I know you agree with me.

Well, Sweetheart, good-night. Tell Frances to kiss you for me.

Affectionately Yrs,

J.B.M.

[1] Evidently she not did say so, but all of her life Mollie was superstitious about starting anything on a Friday.

[2] "La Grippe" is another name for the flu.

Midland, Jan. 19, 1990

My Dear Little Girl,

I don't know that I have written to you any oftener on Sunday than on any other one day. This letter should have been written yesterday, but one of yours I found waiting for me caused my angry passions to arise somewhat and I put off answering for a spell.

I'm not in a good humor yet, but will try to act the Uriah Heep character a few weeks longer.[1] I thought I should not let anything your father said or did affect me any more either one way or the other, but I discover his last state is more exasperating than his first.

His mere disapproval of our plans, further than causing you annoyance and me a few months loneliness, affected me not at all. But when he has come to look on our marriage as a winding up of all your earthly pleasures, that, figuratively speaking, you are committing suicide, that when he attends your wedding he feels, and will very likely act, as if it were your funeral, then I think he is acting in a way that no acquaintance he has ever had with me or any thing he has ever heard about me gives him the least reason in the world to act.

He is making it much harder for you than if he had positively forbidden it in the first place and compelled us to have acted altogether on our own responsibility. I think if you had said in your letter that you would not be more estranged from him than any of *his* other married daughters 'twould have been nearer the mark. I don't think you will ever feel toward him as Cousin Lou feels, because there's hardly a possibility of similar circumstances arising, but I think your visits to his house will be sense of duty visits and will gradually grow like the proverbial angel's.

I think 'twould be a good idea for you to sit down some time and in your imagination draw these two pictures. The one is you and I have been married and are very much in love with each other. You are not living in a very luxurious home, possibly worse than either of us anticipates. Your life is rather monotonous and visits to your father's house are not very pleasant. Dozens of unattractive circumstances arise to which you have heretofore been a stranger. To make up for the unpleasantness, you simply have my affection, which as Capt'n Cuttle would say is "Equaled by few and excelled by none" and a home of which, whether it be a mansion or a cabin, you are the mistress.[2]

The other is, you have written to your father, that you and I will *not* be married. That you prefer being an obedient daughter to marrying a man you love and who loves you, but of whom your father disapproves. That your life in other respects will be similar to what it has been.

I know you think I'm joking when I'd tell you 'twas not too late yet for you to choose the one of the lives you'd prefer, and I know I might as *well* be joking as to give you your choice. But I'm just the same as I was when a year ago I told you I did not want you to marry me unless you were very certain you'd be happy.

You'd have one advantage in choosing the latter. When you had written the imaginary letter to your father, and things were pleasantly arranged once more between you, if you discovered that the old life was not what it was before you knew me, 'twould never be too late while

I was in the land of the living to try the former. You'd be very safe in trusting my love for you to last as long as life does.

I've written quite a letter in getting rid of my ill-humor, but I feel relieved, so that's something.

I was gone nearly all last week and your letters had accumulated to two. I expected another this morning but didn't get it. I'm getting hard to please, am I not?

I was caught out in quite a norther Tuesday night, and a bad cold was the result. I was considerably "under the weather" Friday and yesterday, but feel all right again today.

The man I had with me was rather sick too, so we did not accomplish anything in the way of work. I thought for a long time this new disease, La Grippe, was imagination, but I guess there must be something in it. Nearly everybody has had colds different from the usual form.

I haven't seen the widow since I told you, but if you are going to take to preachers again, I expect I'll have to go back once more to old days. They *do* seem old now, sure enough. I feel as if I'd lived a long time since I used to be on intimate terms with Mrs. Keller.

I've hunted the dictionary through for the spelling of those trees, but Mr. Webster it seems did not know any more about it than I did. At least, I can't find the word. The way it is pronounced in this section is "Catalpa."[3] If this is not right I'm willing to be corrected.

If you will find out for me the address of that publishing firm to which Dr. James sends for books, I will open up communication with it in regard to reading matter. I'm wanting some myself frequently, and had just as well invest in substantial books.

About the cards, I do not know what is best to do. There seem to be more trifling stumbling blocks in the way of our getting married than in similar cases. I could easily send down to Campbell at Lampasas and he would fix them up all right, but the chances are your father would not be suited. I haven't suited him in anything yet except the choice of a wife, and he seems to have some objections there.

Just 7 weeks and 4 days, Little Girl, and our differences will be settled between ourselves.

Ever Aff Yours,
J.B.M.

[1] In Dickens' *David Copperfield*, Uriah Heep is a groveling, " 'umble" character.

[2] Captain Cuttle is a character in Dickens' *Dombey and Son*.

[3] His guess at the spelling is correct. It is in Webster's now.

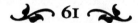 61

Midland, Jan. 21, 1890

My Dear Little Girl,
The remark with which you closed your last letter will do quite well for me to use as a starter, except that it would not do to commence each letter just the same. I would not know what evening I didn't want to see *you*. I don't mean to infer that I think there are some moments when you don't want to see me tho'. I'm resting pretty easy now that I could always add to your happiness by my presence. You see, I have to make love for both of us, but I think this rather an advantage I have over you. Whenever I run out of material, I can tell you for a while how much you are to me, and then remind you gently that I am something to you.

I wonder if two people ever before put as much faith into what the future would do for them when waiting for their wedding as you and I do. I think being engaged without any definite time fixed for the fulfillment must be a nuisance, but I also think that no matter how long the engagement, the day should not be fixed very far in the future. I know that a great many years of my life were wasted before I knew you, but none of them seem to have been so absolutely thrown away as the few weeks since we were in Dallas, Christmas week alone excepted. . . .

Jan. 22. We are having some disagreeable weather in this section but I suppose 'tis the same with you, possibly worse. I don't know but that it makes a person feel better physically than the fore-part of the winter. My health seems to be improving. The only way I can tell this, however, is I eat more and rest easier at night. I haven't dreamed of that other girl any more, so I guess the symptoms are favorable.

I guess from the information from headquarters, that Mch. 13th will be the happy day for us instead of the 14th. This is better than one day later. I wish something would occur now to change the month to one nearer.

I have not found the last three weeks tho' to be slow in passing. How is it with you? It doesn't seem three weeks ago since I told you good-bye the last time. I'm afraid it is more monotonous with you than with me. It's only in looking ahead and imagining how long 7 weeks *can* be that I sometimes get out of patience.

I "kinder" dread, too, the ordeal to you. I feel quite certain 'twill be made rather disagreeable. For my own part now, aside from the fact that I'll be marrying the nicest girl I ever knew, I shall somewhat enjoy the triumph over your father. I trust for your sake he will not try to make things unpleasant, but if he should, I imagine I can get enough amusement out of the situation to keep from feeling very small.

I never was made to feel small yet if I was situated so I could "talk back," but in this case I couldn't. You say its not pretty *to* talk back, but it affords infinite satisfaction at times. I think if you were to try it occasionally you would agree with me.

I should not be giving you this kind of advice tho', because I expect you'll talk back enough in the days to come.

Thad, I should think, was beginning rather early to learn the art of flirting, but I guess he comes by it naturally.* I don't think it would pay in the long run, even if there were no harm done. I imagine if I had carried on the game as long and earnestly as Thad Bell, for instance, I would not feel half as secure in your affection as I do. The mere fact that I had loved dozens of girls before you would keep you anxious. Even if, as you say, you would not want me to marry you if I found one I liked better, still you would not permit yourself to love me near as much if you were not certain there was no chance of my finding another.

So far as a fellow's own conscience goes, [it] does not matter much, but I know Thad would have felt a trifle easier when he married Miss Florence if she had been the only woman he had made love to. If I had written you all this a year ago, I believe I *did tell* you a good-deal of it, you would have been very skeptical. I know you now derive almost as much consolation from the fact that I *did* not tell every girl I met that I loved her, as you do from the conviction that I *do* not now. Then again, if a man were really to fall in love with a woman like you, and lose her because of his reputation as a flirt, I think all of his previous "fun" would be a very poor recompense for the loss.

All the satisfaction I get out of this, however, I know is not equal to yours. You won't flatter me any so I have to flatter myself.

You *have* flattered *me* tho', haven't you, Sweetheart? The greatest compliment a man could pay a woman is to ask her to be his wife, and the greatest compliment she could pay him is to consent, so I guess we are square.

Aff. Yours,
J.B.M.

---

* This refers to Mollie's younger brother, Thad McCormick, who is fifteen years old.

62

Midland, Jan. 25, 1890

My Dear Little Girl,

After your assurance of writing me Sunday, I *have* been disappointed the last two or three days when no letter came. Your resolutions and mine in regard to letter writing seem to go by contraries. I fully resolve *not* to write before a certain time, and very seldom wait until then. You promise to write on a particular day and very frequently put it off. So far as you are concerned, I believe my way suits you best.

Are you mindful of the fact that the letter I got this morning had never been sealed? But as there were no tender passages in it, if anyone had been curious, they could not have accused you of being sentimental.

I see in the *Dallas News* that the "Stern Parent" has been confined to his room with La Grippe. I wonder if the physical indisposition relieved his mind any and his bodily ailments cause any relaxation of the mental depression under which he has been laboring. Or was the reverse the case? If the latter, then I should imagine his wife, if she attended him, would have preferred being at home with her two delicate children, and secretly rejoicing that she would soon have the pleasure of bidding a permanent farewell to her youngest and ironical step-daughter.

Now I guess you are mad. Fortunately, I'm not so afraid of making you mad now as I once was. It gives a fellow lots of satisfaction to feel secure enough in the affection his girl has for him to be able to laugh at her occasionally, and know she values his love too much to be *very* angry at what he says. But then you know I love you far too well, and have too high an opinion of you to tease you much. . . .

Midland, since I came back, has not been very gay. The revivalists had everything their own way until they closed their meetings nearly a week ago. Last night there was a dance out in the country twelve miles, and I think nearly all the society people of the town "took it in." I did not go, but loaned another fellow my buggy, and could have loaned the horses but told him I had conscientious scruples against lending them to anyone unless in cases of emergency. I don't consider a ball a case of this kind, even if a fellow has made a contract to take his girl and has no way.

Mr. Horton's house, just north of us, is under construction. I suppose he will move up from Marienfeld as soon as it can be occupied.

I can't tell what's coming over me, Sweetheart, in the way of writing letters. I did *once* have an idea that I could do moderately well in this line, but my conceit has become a thing of the past. I simply can't write to you now-a-days at all. It's not that the pleasure is any less or that I have any less to say, and so far as liking to get yours, they have become a matter of necessity. But it seems whenever I sit down to write, my first thought is, "Well, this is one more off my hands," and instead of being able to talk to you as I could once, I'm struggling all the time for something to say.

I think you feel very much the same, from the general tone of your late letters, so you will not think I'm getting tired of writing, except in the sense of its taking the place of talking, nor will you think I appreciate yours any less, because I imagine you feel "pretty much" as I do. Neither of us writes from a sense of duty, because if you feel anything like I do, you had rather write to me than to anyone to whom you ever write; you had rather receive my letters than those from any one else.

I know too that if we had been married in Nov. and were separated from each other now, the same distance we are, we could write to each other as easily as we ever did. So the present situation seems to have a demoralizing effect on our letter writing as it does on our tempers sometimes.

Don't propose that we try silence for a while. I'd rather do without any one meal, especially breakfast, than to live without your letters. I know you want mine even if they don't shine as models of composition.

Yours Aff.
J.B.M.

Midland, Jan. 28, 1890

My Dear Little Girl,

I thought possibly I would get a longer letter from you ere this, so did not answer your last, and as I had just mailed you one the day before, I imagined another so soon would prove of a sameness. I guess, however, all I've written to you lately have not been noted for variety. . . .

Time is hanging on my hands at the present time even more heavily than usual. The fellow who has been working for me has been on the sick list since we came in from the ranch more than ten days ago, and I have been simply killing time since. It dies very slowly in one sense and is drifting away very rapidly in another.

I can ill afford to waste it. Still, until I get the ranch supplied with water, I can't make a single move in the way of business.

I don't know that I feel blue over the situation, but when a man starts "down hill" in a financial way, as I did a year and a half ago when I sold out here, it seems almost impossible to find a stopping place. I think now if someone were to offer me a job at barely living wages, I'd take it just to find a breathing spell, and let my employer do my thinking for a while. I hate to work for anyone else, but I imagine 'twould be quite a relief right now to make a machine out of myself for a few months.

I can look back even a short distance and see what ought to have been done. It has been this way for months past. I can't, do what I will, at the time I act, decide on the right thing.

I read somewhere once the method which was used in training fleas. The first thing necessary was to keep them from jumping. They were placed in a glass case with a very low cover, and whenever one made the effort to hop, its head came in contact with the ceiling of its cage. In a short time these lively creatures gave up all ideas of leaving the floor, and for the rest of their lives were contented to crawl.

I feel like I suppose these feel when they have been checked in their movements a few times, but differ in this respect. I'll either break through the roof or have an injured skull in making the attempt.

From the present outlook, my anxiety about leaving you alone frequently thro' April and May was groundless. Unless things change I will be comparatively idle through those months. In one respect, of course, this will be appreciated by both of us. In the respect that, as I say, 'twill be valuable time lost, we may neither of us fancy it so well in the "long run."

From the catalogue you send me of the Library Ass'n, I do not see any benefit to be derived from it unless one is a member. I wrote to them, however, asking information. The address was all I really wanted anyway.

As this will not go before Thursday, I think I'll discontinue for tonight and perhaps I will hear from you tomorrow.

I did not get the expected letter this morning, and as I am going out of town today for a while, I was disappointed. Very likely when I come back I'll find two awaiting for me again, but I should have liked one today.

You can count on my writing as soon as I can, but it may be a week before I return.

Good-bye,
Aff. Yours
J.B.M.

 64

Midland, Feb. 4, 1890

My Dear Little Girl,

. . .The two letters I've read twice today I think are very, very, nice letters. I don't mind in the least your giving vent to your worries, when you write to me, not in the sense of thinking you are of a complaining disposition, of course.

I hate to have you worried, just because I have been fortunate enough to awaken some of your affection. I think I complained enough, and do now sometimes, both at and *to* you to justify you in opening your mind *to* me. You have never yet found fault with my way of doing things, so I do not know when you were inclined to frown on my shortcomings.

I liked the general tone of these two last letters some way. Not that I ever failed to appreciate anything you wrote, but we seem to be drawing closer together, not only as regards time, but to stand out alone as it were from the rest of the world.

So far as I was concerned, it has been this way all along. I had no ties whatever which need be broken by marrying. If in marrying you I would have been compelled to have made any ruptures with anyone, my gain would have more than made up the loss.

With you it has been altogether different heretofore, and in many ways is yet. Judging from these last letters, I believe that not only have you decided that you *ought* to marry the man you love, and who loves you, but aside from this fact, 'twill be rather a relief than otherwise to have only one with whom to differ and agree, be your own "boss" and do as you please generally.

I'm beginning to think possibly all the trouble you've had about marrying me may have been for the best. 'Twill not be near so hard to say good-bye to your old home when it has been made so unpleasant for you lately, as it would have been, had everything been favorable and your father had treated you with kindness up to the last, and shown by his *actions* he was really sorry because you were going, and not simply because I told him I did not need his consent.

I know a home can sometimes be so unpleasant that almost any change is agreeable, and while I've never wished you to marry me on this account, I do not think 'twill be any more likely to make you have "retrospective leanings for what you have left. . . ."

I engaged a man some days ago to place some rocks around and under the back fence, to keep the pigs out, but I suppose he is resting somewhere. I think I remarked before, a great many people in this city like to rest.

I've been taking some rather violent exercise since I wrote you last, using the pick and shovel in a hole in the ground about fifty feet deep. It's fine exercise for developing the muscles, but not very good for softening the hands. I was getting right proud of my hands, too. Thought they would be in elegant shape by March, but I fear this exercise long kept up will not help their appearance much.

Isn't it curious how men's tastes run sometimes. I might have stayed in Lampasas, done nothing but sit at a desk and draw on my imagination a little, slept in a comfortable bed every night and had a well cooked meal three times a day, and possibly made more money in the end than I can here. Instead of that, I'm spoiling my complexion by being out in the sun, sleeping on the ground half the time, eating bread and bacon, cooked out doors, and living in the middle of a "wilderness" even when in town. *Still* I'm moderately happy. . . .

I'll be glad when you feel as much at home here as I do, when you feel like the old life was a thing so far in the past as to be almost a dream. That the life you lead here, while it may be a full of hardships for you as a woman, as it is for me as a man, still I hope when you go "back east" on a visit, you will think, "Well, the plains have their drawbacks, and the eastern town their advantages, but *I* prefer the plains," where the walls are not papered, the dining room is the kitchen, they carry water from the wells, and walk in sandy roads.

When we sigh for a change, we will get on the [railroad] cars, provided we wake up in time, and a few hours will carry us to towns of paved streets and electric lights. We will elbow our way thro' the crowd at the depot to the carriage stand. A few minutes ride and we arrive at the handsome residence on some handsome street.

We go in and are treated with the greatest hospitality. We try our utmost to make ourselves agreeable. In twenty-four hours we wish with all our hearts we were back once more on "the plains" and our visit at an end.

One feature of the city, and only one particularly, I would like convenient, and that is the theatre. But as we have each lived this long with limited opportunities for theatre going, I guess we can "make out" still without it.

Half our time of waiting since I saw you I believe is gone. Five weeks ago tonight we parted, and five weeks more will pass before I see you again. I suppose I shall be there on Tuesday night.

I think very likely my letters to you will necessarily be limited to one a week. Sometimes I may exceed this number, but if I make them all this length, I guess you'll think one sufficient.

I had a communication from the Library Ass'n today saying for a fee of $3.00 I could join that body. I suppose I'll send it.

As you seem to agree with Cousin Lucy in thinking newspaper letters not the best, this one ought to find favor in your sight. I think once or twice I've closed a letter (not to you) with the brilliant remark "nothing more of interest." When a person will consider how little of interest to one who had never been here, is likely ever to take place, this remark might be made at a letter's beginning.

Good-bye, Sweetheart, and if I write to you this much without assuring you of the fact that you are the dearest Little Woman in the world, its not because I forget it for a single line, but I'm afraid I might spoil you in some of your most admirable traits, that of meekness, for one. . . .

I expect tho', my fear is groundless. I had to tell you very, very often that I did love you before you believed it. I guess I might tell you with perfect safety for another year that you were lovable before you'd think so yourself.

After we are together for good I'll try to make you *see* and *feel* that *I* think you are more to be loved than any one *I* ever knew.

Yours Aff.

J.B.M.

65

Midland, Feb. 11. 1890

My Dear Little Girl,

I'm comfortably fixed now for a good long talk, and with no fear of being disputed, at least for a while.

The first thing I heard this morning was a hard north wind blowing, so I thought to myself, this will be too cold today for any work, so I'd have a good excuse for coming to town and reading my little girl's letters, and do a little talking myself.

While I was doing all this thinking one of the tent ropes broke and the structure descended, thereby hastening the "getting up" of my companion and self. Usually to have a tent blow down on a cold night provokes me to wrath, but this morning I did not complain.

One lucky thing I noticed today is having a ranch *north* of town. I can then come home with my *back* to the wind. So whenever I happen to be caught out during a norther, you can look for me home within six or seven hours from the time the wind starts, or by one or two o'clock in the afternoon if the norther commences at night. I *have* driven to town *facing* one to escape sitting over a campfire, but I do not appreciate this particularly.

I guess I'm somewhat of your mind when away from me-and if I'm in such a hurry to come in after your *letters*, what will it be when I can know that *you* in person will be here. . . .

I never fully realize until I'm away from you for a while the utter impossibility of my doing without you. I'd marry you on the 13th ult. if I *knew* you had been in the habit of telling your escorts or callers good-night the same way you tell me. I believe, tho', my love for you is such that I would not let you marry me did I not think you'd be happy.

The weeks glide along quite rapidly with me. I trust time does not hang very heavily on your hands. March 13th is not very far off now, and then —

I think neither of us ever considers a single day after that, but I trust we will have a great many to consider, and then when we are both old, we can look back and still think we did not really begin life until our wedding day.

I was reading a novel the other day, *Very Hard Cash*. I began it before Christmas. In it is the following, "We men are all alike, we are never satisfied unless we know our sweethearts are miserable too, this consoles us." It came in where a fellow was accusing his girl of bad treatment, not realizing that she was suffering too.

I think since I discovered that you were not reveling in contentment over affairs in general, that I have felt much better. I see that I've written considerable in this letter which might lead you to think I was feeling blue, but I do not. I'm feeling in very good spirits at the present time, nothing to make me so, particularly, except hard work, and most of that thrown away.

The old theory that water "seeks a level," "flows down hill" and all such stuff, I've proved to my own *dis*satisfaction is incorrect. I have sunk three holes in the ground all *below* a level with the water in surrounding wells, and the fluid absolutely refuses or fails to run into any of my openings. I began a fourth yesterday and intend to go back as soon as the weather moderates and continue operations.

I send you a clipping from the *Lampasas Leader*. I can't exactly understand whether Uncle James quoted from some one else or if some one has been borrowing from him. I think the same or nearly the same is claimed by his family as being one of his productions. This is just one from half a column of a like kind of literature. I do not take the *Leader*, but Mr. Campbell has sent me the last few numbers.

I trust you will not feel very lonesome until I write again.

Goodnight.
Aff. Yours.
J.B.M.

[Enclosure]
There is a word of plural number
A foe to ease and peaceful slumber,
To almost any word you take
And add an s you plural make,
But if you add an s to this
Great is the metamorphosis,
Plural is plural now no more
And that becomes sweet that was bitter before.
Ans. Cares-caress.

Midland, Feb. 23, 1890

My Dear Little Girl,

Letter writing may be a poor excuse for conversation, but I know when I haven't seen a letter from you for so long, nor written to you, it makes me feel almost like I was meeting you after an absence when I finally receive yours, and try to answer them. I know you are getting impatient for one now, but I only came in town today, and did not have time to get this off in tomorrow's mail.

I intend to be in Midland now until I go to Graham, so I will not make you wait so long again for a letter, at least before the 13th of March.

I guess if you had been here when I came in, you would not have owned me even as a cousin. I was rather a rough looking customer. My clothes were well covered with different kinds of soil accumulated from the surface of the ground to a depth of several feet below it, and my face and hands were similar. However, I turned on the water, built a fire in the cook stove, and soon had this bath tub in working order. So now, while I'm not a dude, I do feel somewhat more respectable.

I guess this well on which I've been working will prove a success. I had the hole *bored* last fall, but from some cause the workmen could not keep the sand from filling it up. There is plenty of water when I reach it, and I'm much nearer than ten days ago. I've been digging directly around the *bored* well, and found it very encouraging to once or twice every day take the cloth from out this opening and look down at the water, plainly visible several feet below.

As I said, I shall not go back again but send someone back in my stead. Laying all joking aside, I can't afford to have my hands in the shape they are now when they are joined to yours. Then too, I have some fixing up to do here.

I've had a carpenter at work on your dining room, and that is now nearly finished, that is, the woodwork. I shan't have any painting or oiling done to it until you come. You will be the best judge of how you'd like it. I haven't fully decided if I shall put down the carpets before you come. When I came back today the floor was almost covered with sand, and 'twill be this way until April. The two front rooms on the east side are not so bad, but even they were rather dusty.

If you can stand Midland for the first two or three weeks after you try it, then I shall have hopes you will like it in time. It's possible the sandstorms may cease sooner than April this year, for your benefit, but I'm inclined to think not.

After I put a hose on the pipes so we can keep the ground damp, the dust may not be so bad around the house. Anyway, I expect from the frame of mind you are in at present, you would consider sweeping the floors of this mansion, and rubbing sand from your eyes no worse than being sympathized with for anticipating it.

I'm doing all this complaining for you. I know you'll not do it for yourself, even when you see what it is. For my part I've become so accustomed to it, that unless it actually interferes with some work I have on hand, I mind the wind very little.

I expect 'twould be a good idea for you, if you can, to beg of your neighbors and friends some rose-bush cuttings that you care to have, if 'twill not be too late to put them out after the middle of Mch. Its hard to get anything you want in that line after you get here. I've been intending all the time to plant something of the kind myself, but have had very little time to attend to it since Christmas. I would prefer, too, you

*Sandstorm over Midland, Texas, February 20, 1894. Courtesy Midland County
Historical Museum.*

should arrange everything about the house and yard to suit yourself,
because even if my arrangements met with *your* approval, I know your
taste would be much better than mine. I think "fixins" on the *out*side
of a house ought to a certain extent appear well to passers by.

I do not envy you if your father comes home much before you leave.
I expect he and you will come to an open rupture before the wind up.
I never have had much idea the affair would come off peaceably. I guess
'twill be much better if I do not show myself much before Thursday
morning.

Of course, I will have to see you. I couldn't stay in the same town
from Tuesday evening until the 13th and not see you, but I do not know

how much more unreasonableness I can put up with and not "talk back." 'Twould be a great pity to spoil the friendly (!) understanding (!) existing at the present time between Judge McCormick and myself, when you and I had put ourselves out so much to obtain it, by talking back at the last moment.

I haven't the same restraint upon me now that I had last summer and fall. Then I was afraid of losing you, but since I realize you are not very anxious to get lost, and think you love me as I do you, and know I wouldn't give *you* up if you were to "sass" every relative *I* have in the world, I haven't the control over my meek and gentle spirit I once had.

I guess I can hardly accept the Dr.'s invitation to call again *before* the 13th, but will likely impose on him then for a while.

I will send the sample card to Lampasas and tell Mr. Campbell to send them to you when printed. In the meantime I will make out a list of names from Midland, and send you. I will start from here on the 9th and do not care to have any cards reach here until after I leave.

I know this is not much of a letter to send you in reply to yours, but this is all the paper I have on hand and very likely I will feel like talking to you again in a day or two, so for the present, good-night.

Ever Aff Yours,

J.B.M.

Monday.

I had the letter written last night all ready for the P.O. but read your last this morning, so I secured some more paper and will try to continue. If I repeat anything in this you will likely think either my memory is failing or I have very little impression made upon it by what I write you.

I'm glad you are having a good time, and hope it will not hang very heavy. So often it's the case when the young men of a town know a girl is spoken for, [they] give her up entirely. That, while 'twould not worry a woman much, still she occasionally feels a little dull. I know Austin to be a great place for this, and I guess Miss Florence often missed going out while Thad was away. If Graham had been the same, your case would have been rather hard when I would not have been on hand at all.

I don't think we have gotten quite as much satisfaction out of our *engagement* as people generally seem to. But as is often the case at other times, I discover myself almost forgetting the unpleasant passages, and remembering those which have been far more happy than another other part of my life. I know if I were to commence 12 months ago, and count the days since then which have been free from worry of any kind, and those which have been full of it, the completely happy days would be in the minority.

Still, taking today as a point of observation, and looking back for a period of years, when month after month would go by without a cloud, I think the few happy moments I have lived during the last eight months, would stand out so plainly in view and be so weighted down with pure and entire happiness as to throw in the shadow all my other years of existence, be they free from cares or the reverse.

I think such will be the case when we have lived together a number of years. Not that the happy days will be limited to a few, but that worries of different kinds will appear obscure and far away when they are gone. Many, many moments will come when our happiness in each other's affection will be so entire that our lives before we were married, or loved each other, can not be recalled with clearness.

As is nearly always the case when waiting for a certain time, the last few days seem to be the longest, but they will pass. While we may not be wholly responsible for what comes afterwards, I think if we do not make each other the companions we both expect, the fault will be our own.

I do not dread the ordeal particularly. Speed is the point upon which we must both insist, more so in Mch., than in Nov. Whether it be a failing or otherwise, I've never learned to look on getting married with the same amount of seriousness that people usually do, that is, a mournful kind of seriousness.

When a man and woman make their promises to each other, the serious part of the affair is over, so far as they are concerned. As for others, be they mothers, fathers, brothers or sisters, I think they have nothing in the world to do with it, further than general custom allows.

I know this theory is the great stumbling block between your father and me, but I have as much right to think my way as he has his. He had a perfect right to try to persuade you to give me up and I had the same right to try to talk you into marrying me. If you had told me or written me something like this, "I love you but cannot marry you without my father's consent," I would have known quite well that you did not love me well enough to marry me at all.

I did certainly know you much better than he did, if he ever thought he could induce you to break promises made me. It certainly was a mistake at the start to be so independent, but I did not know him quite so well then.

Good-bye again,
Aff.
J.B.M.

Midland, Feb. 28, 1890

My Dear Little Girl,

If I don't hurry up it will be a week again before you get another letter from me, and this time I will have no excuse whatever.

I have been in town since I wrote last and find the change from camp very agreeable, especially yesterday and today, when a cold norther has been blowing.

I'm getting tired keeping house alone tho'. Except in bad weather I believe I prefer the ranch to town the way things are now. I think I've discoursed before, however, on the degrees of loneliness, and that being in a house by yourself was the comparative degree.

I've been making some alterations tho', inside and out, and keeping busy. The time passes well enough. Yesterday was too cold to work, as has been most of today. Tomorrow very likely our weekly or semi-weekly sandstorm will come and I will get another day's rest, unless I find employment inside.

I was reminded a few days ago of what may be our fate on account of the dust. One of Marienfeld's citizens moved up to Midland into a new house just completed (this is not Mr. Horton) and I think has not been here more than two weeks. A few days ago he sold out, saying his wife couldn't possibly stand the dust.

As Marienfeld is only eighteen miles from here, and no wind-breaks of any kind between, I thought some imagination must have been indulged in. He is to still occupy his place for two months, and by then the chances are this country will be an earthly paradise, without any draw-back whatever.

I don't mean that you are likely to want to move *quite* this soon. If you were one of the women who do not know what they want, I guess I should have discovered the fact long ago. I might say right here, for your future reference, you know, that the only class of women that I *particularly* can't endure are those whose traits here on earth would lead one to suppose they would find something lacking in heaven.

I expect very likely tho' I love you so well that if you *were* to disclose after a while characteristics of this kind, I'd never think you were drawing on your imagination.

I sometimes think I write to you almost too unreservedly. For instance, the foregoing might prevent you at times of expressing your ideas of things that were a real grievance. But you understand me well enough, I trust, to know I'm not trying at this stage of the game to educate you to *my* ideas.

Worse and worse. I've made three explanations now, and each one is worse than what I wrote first and needs explaining itself. I'll just remark "present company excepted" and subside.

I think your dining room is going to be, according to your notion, the nicest room in the house when completed. 'Twould be a pity if a house this size didn't have *one* respectable looking room. I hope we will not find much wrong with this one.

Sweetheart, I can't write this evening. I'll see you D.V.* in less than two weeks, and the same old feeling of looking forward some way prevents my thinking of writing. Very likely I'll conclude our little romance (as regards correspondence) with some sort of a letter next week. For this time, farewell.

Yrs. Aff.
J.B.M.

I send you a list of names to whom to send cards. If not in the regulation style to send cards to unmarried men, you can leave out such. Please don't mail any to Midland before Friday next.

J.B.M.

* D.V. Deo volente. God willing.

68

Midland, March 4, 1890

My Dear Little Girl,

I guess this will be the closing chapter of our little love tale. I believe nearly all novels close when the principal characters marry. Curious, isn't it? The most interesting part of a story to *others* ends when the most interesting part to the *two chiefly* concerned begins. So no doubt will be ours.

If we either cared for notoriety in an affair of this kind, I think in a moderate way we should be satisfied. For a while, I suppose, after we get home, *your* folks will be anxious to know how things are, and the Midlanders will be anxious to satisfy their curiosity. Then the anxiety we have created, throughout *half* of Texas anyway, will subside.

Left to ourselves we will endeavor to demonstrate to all our interested friends, and realize the fact very thoroughly ourselves, that the first part of the story in which we have figured needs no sequel to record our mishaps and misfortunes, our disagreements and reconciliations. Our lives will flow very smoothly, interesting only to each other.

That if "perchance in some succeeding year" some writer were to take our engagement as a foundation upon which to build his romance, he could bring it to a close on our wedding day with the remark truthfully made, "They lived happy ever afterwards."

As *one* individual's life is generally what he or she makes it, so I think is the life or lives a husband and wife live. I think we both love each other far too well to ever be compelled to bring logic to our assistance to enable us to put up with unknown traits (unknown to each other now) which may show themselves hereafter. I think we are both reasonable, and if one or both of us should prove different from what the other imagines, I do not think 'twould lessen our mutual affection.

As I've frequently said before, if such a thing be possible, I love you far too well to be *always* as happy as I might be if my affection was more moderate. As I remarked in my letter the one before the last, many moments will come when everything else will be so completely blotted out by a sense of perfect contentment, that my life will be a very fair average.

While it may sound a trifle conceited, I'm inclined to fear the same thing for you. You see my ideas of you have undergone quite a change. I thought a year ago you'd be unhappy because you didn't love enough. Now I'm afraid you'll love me too much.

If we were not to be separated often, I don't think, except in case of sickness, our excess of affection would cause us any anxiety. As it will inevitably be, we'll both feel rather lonesome sometimes. However, we need not anticipate trouble.

I could not tell from your letter how sick you had been, but sincerely trust you are well again. The same old presentiment came over me when I read it, that we would once more be disappointed. It hasn't bothered me lately. 'Twould look like fate if one or the other shouldn't be able to go through with the ceremony on the 13th, wouldn't it?

If anything does happen tho', Little Sweetheart, you'll find in me a second Jacob as regards perseverance. But I'm not very desirous of following the example of that celebrated shepherd. Eight more days will decide for us and unless I'm worse off bodily than I have been within twenty years, I will be on hand.

I was intending to leave here Sunday, but think now I may not start before Monday. I suppose the best plan would be to get a team and buggy in Weatherford to make the trip each way. If I do not go down before Monday, I will not be in Graham before Wednesday afternoon.

I will see if I can get a permit from the County Clerk by proxy, and if so will write Dr. James to attend to it for me, so I'll have nothing to do but interview the minister. While I agree with you that I think there will be no unpleasantness between your father and myself, 'twill save us both twenty-four hours of acting if I do not come to G. until Wednesday.

I do not know, of course, whether 'twould be better to go to your house or to Cousin Lou's, but would prefer taking my chances at the latter. I suppose we can see very little of each other alone before we leave, but I guess we can make it up hereafter.

I will try to have something to eat on hand when we get home. I'll be this much advanced from Nov. anyway.

I hope you will be well as ever when this reaches you, Little Girl. Take good care of yourself until I have a chance to perform that duty myself.

Goodnight.
Aff. Yours,
J.B.M.

John Barclay McGill in Mexico. Date of photograph is unknown.

Epilogue

After a few years in Midland, and the birth of three girls, one of whom they lost, JBM and Mollie moved to central Mexico, to a ranch he bought. In 1904 they had another daughter, my mother. Three years later a ranch worker came to the house in the middle of the day with the message that my grandfather was dead, apparently of a heart attack. Mollie returned to Texas and the domination of her father.

Agnesa Reeve